Optimize

7 Simple Steps to Nurture Your Heart

This Positivity Pulse Action Guide is a quick start implementation guide for
The Nurtured Heart Approach® **for use with adults**

Alletta Bayer & Sherry Blair

Visit **SherryBlairInstitute.com** for additional information, free downloads, and resources.

Copyright © 2016 Alletta Bayer & Sherry Blair

Shakti Publishing

All rights reserved.

ISBN-13: 978-1530420032

ISBN-10: 1530420032

DO NOT DUPLICATE OR DISTRIBUTE WITHOUT WRITTEN PERMISSION.

This copyrighted electronic or physical publication is a personal workbook and is intended exclusively for use by an individual for their own use or by individuals in a training program, which is led by a Sherry Blair Institute for Inspirational Change approved facilitator. This workbook, either electronic or physical, in its whole or any part thereof may not be forwarded or duplicated singly or for use in a classroom or other group setting or online or for use as part of a training program without written permission. Such use may be only be granted by Sherry Blair Institute for Inspirational Change in a written agreement and upon payment of applicable fees. For information on bulk sales or becoming a facilitator please email optimize@sherryblairinstitute.com.

Character Illustrations by Brenda Brown at www.webtoon.com
Graphics Creatively by Kristine Requena

DEDICATION

We dedicate this book to all the beautiful people we have served. Your love and light ignites us to burn more brightly.

CONTENTS

Acknowledgements..i

Welcome Letter..3

Guide to Success...4

Two Secrets..5

OPTIMIZE Activity 1:   **Prepare:** Are You Ready to Change?......................................15

OPTIMIZE Activity 2:   **Mindset**: Open to Experience Yourself & Others.......................31

OPTIMIZE Activity 3:   **Build**: Nurture Heart® Foundations..51

OPTIMIZE Activity 4:   **Support**: Three Stands™ that Support the Methods....................73

OPTIMIZE Activity 5:   **Discover**: Strategies to Support the Stands................................91

OPTIMIZE Activity 6:   **Accelerate**: Strategies to Spiral Positivity..................................111

OPTIMIZE Activity 7:   **Reset to OPTIMIZE:** Strategies to Get You Back On Track.............123

ACKNOWLEDGMENT

We would like to acknowledge the inspiration that Howard "Howie" Glasser, the creator of The Nurtured Heart Approach®, has been to both of us.

Sitting in a one day NHA training, Alletta realized in the first hour this was the missing piece she needed to help her daughter's teacher turn around some attention-getting behavior. And as the day unfolded she became more and more excited as she realized not only would she be a better parent, but she would now be able to use the NHA to help her clients build Inner Wealth®, develop positive relationships and thrive in any environment.

Sherry was so on fire after a long and energizing week getting certified as an Advanced Trainer in the NHA® in Arizona that she ended up writing her first book for NHA in the workplace on the plane home from Phoenix, AZ to Newark, NJ. She wrote on the backs of papers and cocktail napkins for hours and couldn't wait to get back to changing the world with this amazing approach which she realized would be like adding Miracle Grow™ to the clients and families she served in New Jersey.

We are also grateful to Howie because he inadvertently brought us together at the Certification week in Arizona and later recruited us to serve on the First NHA Global Summit Committee, where we developed a deep friendship and a collaborative working relationship that is still blossoming.

Thank you, Howie, for your service and dedication to changing lives by nurturing success, for bringing us together, and for inspiring us to help make the world a more positive place, one great recognition at a time!

The content of this self-coaching guide is directly inspired and grounded in Howard Glasser's book, *Igniting Greatness*.

Optimize

WELCOME TO THE FIRST DAY OF THE REST OF YOUR LIFE

Maybe you're looking for just a little more positive energy and good will in your relationships with others. Perhaps you feel you're "almost there" and with just a little more "something" you could flourish. Or maybe you're feeling so much negativity overall lately, and you would really like to discover how to turn that around. Whatever your motivation, this self-coaching action guide is for you. Step by step, this guide will teach you how to energetically nurture yourself so that you may grow and flourish. Doing the simple exercises will empower you to become the person you want to be.

As you work with intention through the exercises and incorporate your new skills into your daily life, you will be amazed as you observe the changing quality of your relationship with yourself and even with others. You may sense a new "lightness," or what we call a *Positivity Pulse*, in your relationships at home, work and play.

We designed this guide to take you on a journey of self-discovery. There might be times during this journey when you find yourself wanting to skip an exercise or change things around. Don't! If you come up against these desires, that's when it's important to stick with the process because often times the areas in which you want to spend the least amount of time and energy are *exactly* the areas where you need more understanding or are the weakest and need the most practice. By allowing us to guide you on this journey you will experience incredible results.

Working through each exercise in order builds a strong foundation for positive change and personal transformation. Each week as you learn and practice new skills, you will be building an upward spiral of positivity, leading to an expansive, flourishing life. As so often in life, the more you practice, the better you get.

And that's what this self-coaching guide is ultimately about: **POSITIVE RESULTS**.

Commit. *Practice.* Transform and *Optimize*

To your personal success,
Alletta & Sherry

GUIDE TO SUCCESS

Here are some suggestions for working the exercises of your Action Guide.

1. **Work through the entire workbook in order.** The program is designed in sequential exercises with each step building upon the previous one.

2. **Complete each section and relentlessly practice** as if your life depends upon it.

Remember: *No Practice = No Change*.

3. **Don't skip over the worksheets.** They are designed to help you broaden your perspective and incorporate the learning.

4. **Use the Journal and Worksheet pages** to give you the opportunity to explore topics, find clarity, and deepen your experience. You can choose to type them in the electronic version or handwrite them in the book.

5. **Set and attend regular in-person, phone or online meetings if you are working on the Action Guide with a group or a coach, and be sure to complete each section prior to your meetings.**

6. **If practicing the methods feels a little strange to you at first, congratulations!** Feeling a little (or a lot) out of your comfort zone means you are stretching—and learning new, positive habits.

7. **Grab an accountability buddy** to practice with to stretch into those new ways of being.

Remember (again!): *No Practice = No Change*.

8. **Use your Assessment Worksheet and Personal Surveys** to track your progress.

TWO SECRETS

In a world awash with information and suggestions on what people could or should be doing to be happier and lead more fulfilling lives, many people keep reaching for something new to learn with the hope that they will finally achieve what they are looking for. Recognizing this continuous search for something "out there" is largely ineffective, we believe that the two secrets for leading a happier and more fulfilling life are really quite simple and come from within yourself: you need to determine **what to stop doing** and **how to substitute positive change** to optimize your life. In other words, as Sherry Blair likes to say:

"Stop the freaking insanity!"

But stop what? And how?

The "what" to stop and the "how" is what this book is all about. It is our mission to ignite flourishing qualities and experiences by teaching people **how to identify and stop** what is not working and **how to substitute positive change** in order to create the self-nurturing relationship and experiences you desire. In our work we often use a "pulse line" or heartbeat symbol to express the variety of energy pulse possible for individuals in any setting at home, work or play. To illustrate this concept in the extremes, a "flat-lined" pulse indicates a disengaged and failing pulse, better known as "flat-lining" or perhaps depressed and cynical. A frenetic pulse indicates stressed and crazed energy. Conversely, a robustly beating steady pulse, what we call a "Positivity Pulse," indicates happy, productive, flourishing energy and engaged momentum in a positive direction.

Flat-Line "Zombie" Pulse
(Negative energy: depressed, sad, disengaged, barely functioning, etc.)

Frenetic "Crazed" Pulse
(Negative energy: stressed, resentful, overwhelmed, chaotic, angry, etc.)

Positivity Pulse
(Positive energy: engaged, happy, productive, flourishing, etc.)

We now use a saying we learned from the airlines to describe this idea: "...Put your oxygen mask on first in order to help those around you." And we will be teaching you "how" to do this, how to nurture your *own* greatness and create a "**Positivity Pulse**."

Through doing the exercises in this guide you will learn how you can identify your areas of negativity, the "what to stop," and how to "reset" into positive change. Pay close attention to your "Inner Pulse" in the form of energy that you feel, both positive and negative as you progress, and substitute positive thoughts and behaviors with the strategies we'll teach you to help you Optimize and flourish.

Unhealthy negativity lurks in many forms and all of them are hazardous to your health and well-being.

- **Disgruntled with an overall bad attitude, and low morale.**
- **Disengaged in life, apathetic**
- **A feeling of shrinking or loneliness, not wanting to engage with others**
- **Internal conflict and arguing with others**
- **Feeling sick or *being* sick quite regularly**
- **Just giving your minimum effort**
- **An inability to experience joy or appreciation**

Since negativity has an energetic quality to it, if the negativity were to stop, there would be a big energy void to fill. If this talk of energy sounds "woo-woo" to you, just stop and think for a moment. When someone is acting out in a negative way, how does that make you feel? In descriptive American slang terms, you might say they are a "downer." That is the perfect way to describe negativity in one word, because negative energy is a contagious downer. It brings everyone "down" a few notches in energy level.

And it's difficult, if not impossible, to keep bringing your best efforts and creativity in any setting—as a partner/spouse, a parent, a friend, or co-worker when you continuously experience your own or others' negative energy.

Conversely, when someone expresses excitement about something in a positive way, you might say they are "upbeat." You can feel this because positive energy is also contagious, and even just one happy, excited person positively affects the energy of everyone receiving their positive energy and communications. (Fredrickson, 2009) It has been revealed by Barbara Fredrickson, Keenan Distinguished Professor in the Department of Psychology at the University of North Carolina Chapel Hill, a guru in the study of positive emotions, that energetically *we are indeed changing at the cellular level when we increase positivity*. That's because positivity raises the level of the hormone oxytocin, which ignites more brainpower and gives us that "feel good" energy that also increases our overall well-being. (Fredrickson, 2013)

The health benefits of positive thinking

As cited by the Mayo Clinic, researchers continue to explore the effects of positive thinking and optimism on health. Health benefits that positive thinking may provide include:

- Increased life span
- Lower rates of depression
- Lower levels of distress
- Greater resistance to the common cold
- Better psychological and physical well-being
- Reduced risk of death from cardiovascular disease
- Better coping skills during hardships and times of stress
- Overall higher satisfaction

Now you need the second "secret," in order to feel OPTIMIZED and to get a Positivity Pulse so you hum along like a finely tuned instrument in your relationship with yourself and others. The second secret is learning *how* to fill that energy void left from removing negative energy by substituting the higher energy of positivity. Conscientiously working and practicing the exercises in this book will empower you to implement the "how." It's easy when you go step-by-step. Easy doesn't mean that it isn't hard work—it is a lot of work—but so worth it!

The choice is simple and the choice is yours. You can transform to a happier and more engaged person who is flourishing. And your relationships can become happier and more positive and fulfilling. It all begins with a decision to learn and practice new habits.

> "In this moment, you get to decide.
> Remember, today is the first day
> of the rest of your life and
> this is your moment."
> ~sherry blair

Optimize

Optimize

ACTIVITY 1
Prepare:
Are You Ready to Change?

OPTIMIZE: *7 Simple Steps to Nurture Your Heart* is about empowering you to create an upward spiral of positive feelings, self-love and self-appreciation in everyday activities. Living a flourishing life -- a fuller, richer, happier, more expansive life—that's what it's all about.

Activity 1 Objectives

- To realize the power to change is within you
- To understand the specific keys to successful change
- To understand preparing for change is necessary to achieve success
- To learn the keys to successfully prepare for change
- To state a clear intention of what you want to change

Activity 1 Summary

- Research shows us 40% of who we are is attributable to our intentional activities

- You need a clear vision in order to change – a vision that connects the outward vision of what you "see" in your head connected with the wisdom and yearning of the heart.

- Your passion is one of the most important components of change.

How Ready Are You?

Congratulations on beginning this new and exciting journey! We are honored and happy to be your guides as you learn to nurture your heart and spiral up your positivity. We recognize it can be hard to change as adults when you have spent years thinking, feeling and behaving in the same ol', same ol' ways. But hey! It is possible! When you engage the passion of your heart and the power of your mind and connect them to your reason for changing, you're unstoppable.

But first we have some questions that only you can answer.
- How ready are you for change?
- Were you given this book or did you choose it yourself?
- Did it speak strongly to you or were you just curious?
- Do you have a burning, all-consuming need to change?

Your answers can help you determine the strength of your passion and commitment to your own personal development. So, before you read further, rate yourself from 0 – 100 on these:

0=not at all   **50=take it or leave it**   **100=I need/want it badly**

I have a *reason* and a *need* to change. _____.

My *passion* to grow and nurture my heart is _____.

My *commitment* to learning and practicing the Activities is _____.

My *belief* that I can grow and change and optimize is _____.

Now that you have taken some base measurements, dive in and see if you can notch 'em up!

The Power to Change

If we offered you an honest to goodness, real-life deal of a 40% return on your investment, would you take it? Many promises of enormous return prove to good to be true, but we hope you'll be as excited as we were when we learned that studies show **40% of who we are is due to our intentional activities**, and that means **you have the power to change!**

So many people argue that negative life events, traumatic experiences, maladaptive behaviors and the experience of dysfunctionality in someone's life has a greater impact on who they are than the genes they were born with. Anyone who has struggled to pull themselves out of negative circumstances, as we have, can attest to the fact that it is *hard*.

And then there are those with the opposite opinion who believe that our genes have the greatest impact on who we are. But both of those beliefs *completely* leave out consideration of personal decision and the personal power to change, and that is where Sonya Lyubomirsky and her colleagues' research comes in.

So...what did Lyubomirsky's data indicate? Our genetics, what our biological parents donated to us through their egg and sperm, are responsible for 50% of who we are. Life events contribute 10%, and **40% of who we are is due to our intentional activities!** Wow that's deep! That's the most profound research we've come across to support your quest for personal development.

The bottom line and what we are shouting about here is that **YOU have the POWER TO CHANGE** even more than you might have known before you read this. So use this information to empower yourself, kick up your excitement level a few notches and KNOW your efforts to nurture your heart and Optimize your life can work.

Now, having come this far, what more can you do to make sure your efforts *will* work?

Let's continue by exploring some vital roadmaps for change. We want to give you the benefit of our combined years of study and the hundreds of thousands of dollars we have invested and the best tools possible to ensure your success step by step as you work through these upcoming activities.

Preparation to Change

John Kotter, from Harvard Business School, has studied change for decades and found *70% of change initiatives fail in businesses because there is not enough preparation from the participants.*

Individuals fail, too, when they have not prepared themselves for change. It's not enough for you just to say: "I want to do this." For you to be successful in *your* change initiative you need to prepare and maintain passion and work your way through each of the following *Keys to Successful Change*.

You have to have a powerful need for changing. How will you benefit? What would happen if you don't change? Will there be anyone else affected if you do or don't change? Look at all the angles you can find.

You need to ready yourself for change, gather your thoughts, feelings, passion **AND DECIDE TO START.** You have to want it. You have to want it bad. How bad? BAD! Just a teeny desire won't sustain you, you have to want it BAD!

You need to move from just having an idea about your need or desire to change into marshaling your resources, figuring out how you can make it happen, getting excited, looking at the steps necessary to get you what you want and making a plan, in other words: **PREPARE FOR CHANGE!**

KEYS TO SUCCESSFUL CHANGE

Establish Urgency

Ask yourself these questions:

- How urgently do you want this?

- What is at stake if you don't change?

- Can you afford to wait around to start? Or are you ready to jump into immediate action?

- Are you yawning as you read this or are you lapping up every word, anxious to get started?

Think of how you'll feel when you're learning and growing through these activities and nurturing your heart. You'll be spiraling up your positivity and Optimizing at the same time.

A key to raising your sense of urgency is to lower your complacency. This is a great word loaded with a heavy weight to pull you down if you have it in your life. Let's check out how Merriam defines complacency:

1. a feeling of being satisfied with how things are and not wanting to try to make them better; a complacent feeling or condition

2. self-satisfaction especially when accompanied by unawareness of actual dangers or deficiencies

3. an instance of usually unaware or uninformed self-satisfaction

YUK! Does that sound like any way you want to be? It feels like being rolled in sludge and then trying to run a marathon. Get complacency OUT OUT OUT! by getting your URGENCY and your POSITIVITY UP UP UP!

You'll also want to get any unhealthy negativity OUT as well. You know, anything lurking around to throw cold water on your good intention. If you have any negative people in your life who try and keep you from growing and achieving, DON'T share this with them. Seek out positive people who will support you in your change process.

Believe in *yourself*.
Believe in *your* power to change.
Think about *your* why and *your* urgency.
Don't procrastinate!
Dive in!

> **"Your vision will become clear only when you look into your heart. Who looks outside, dreams. Who looks inside awakens."**
>
> **~ Carl Jung**

This quote is a great reminder to engage your whole self in the process of change. It is so true. If you are always just about external things, about the way things "look," then you might just be looking and imagining in your head. You really need to combine the thoughts in your head with the passion in your heart in order to be able to *take action* to accomplish your intention.

Clarity of Intention

It is important to know what you want before you can take action to make it happen. Otherwise, without knowing clearly what you want, you can't determine the first step to getting started.

Intention is one of the most powerful forces in life you can harness. Sometimes in the early stages of imagining what you want you might have only a vague idea or desire. If you desire clarity but are having a difficult time figuring out what that is—don't worry. This is the time to dream and to imagine different possibilities. You might even feel you can't find a solid idea or a direction to latch onto. Some people describe it as a feeling of swimming around in a deep pot of soup. This "swimming in the soup" can actually be very useful. In fact, some people find they must spend time in this stage of imagining while they are trying to find clarity or while they are exploring different options. But be aware that a pattern of remaining vague after evidence or options are weighed can sabotage your forward motion of change, leading to confusion, inertia, and just plain being STUCK. A pattern of vagueness or indecision may even be an attempt to control the situation by not setting a clear intention or taking action.

An intention can be long-term or short-term. It can be something for everyday or even every moment. It can be about something in particular or about a quality in life or a way of being. It could be something as simple as deciding to write down 3 things that you want to recognize yourself for each day, or it could be longer term such as deciding to change your career by a certain date. Whatever your intention might be, it is important to state it so that you can focus your attention, take action, and measure your success.

When you set and state an intention,
you are making it clear to yourself what you want to do.

What is Your Why?

What is the reason you have invested in this book now?

What is your reason for wanting to nurture your heart now?

How badly do you want it?

Ask yourself when did you start to feel that there was a reason or need to change and write it here:

You must have already gone through that step because here you are, working through the first Activity in this program.

And from the question when? comes what? is it you want to work on. Write your what? here:

And then of course, what is your why? Why now, why does it matter to you at this time of your life?

How will you benefit? Write your why? here:

For anything we undertake to accomplish, there is a why. And the more passionate we are about our why? and why now? the easier it is for us to muster and sustain the energy to do it. Just look back on your life and remember other times when you set about to make changes in your life. Why was it so important for you to start your change process?

Knowing

Knowing is the next step. In order to change, you need to know where you are and where you want to go. Define this for yourself. Some people find it is helpful to write about it in a journal. (We'll show you how in a few pages if you are unfamiliar with that concept.)

Is your journey a straight line from A to B? Some people don't see it as a straight line – some people see it as a winding path. For others, it's circular in which they are starting at a point, and expanding outward. Part of envisioning your journey is to, as we say, chunk it down, into pieces or steps you can do one at a time so you won't get overwhelmed by the complexity of the whole.

What do you think your journey will look like?

Feel like?

Be like?

What has to happen for you to know you are changing?

One thing for sure: Change is a process, not a switch you can flip. Even little things, like coloring your hair. It's not as simple as snapping your fingers. You still have to go through the process of several steps before you can see the new you.

Timeframe

The next important step is Timeframe. Well, since we know you are reading/listening to this, can we assume you have started? Or not. Have you committed to working through the activities? IN ORDER?! Yes, it does take time, AND you need to start here in the beginning and work through each activity as each step moves you further into the upward spiral of positivity and self-nurturing.

So, set your stake in the ground. This is important. Decide to begin. Get that stake out and put it in the ground right now! Mark your calendar with a start date and a finish date. Commit to moving along toward the new you!

Honor Yourself

What's achievement without celebration? Achievement is so much more fun (and sustainable!) when you honor and celebrate yourself as you move through the Activities. Don't wait till the end. That's so masochistic! Spiral up your enthusiasm and your passion by celebrating each step along the way. You don't have to wait for the Reflections at the end of each Activity. Every time you find yourself practicing your new skills you can recognize yourself for making positive changes. And since our brains are "wired" for doing things the same way, each time you do or say or think something differently you are leaving your old patterns behind and laying down new tracks, building new habits and voila! Changing for the better!

Even though this is a guide to show you how to nurture your heart, and not about physical self – care, there is nothing to keep you from throwing in some lavish helpings of that! Why not include special "me" time to celebrate completion of another activity, or make it a game that for every 10 times you recognize yourself you get points to do something like take a bubble bath, check your social media, get some exercise, whatever will keep your enthusiasm and positivity up.

You get the picture. Make it fun! Celebrate!

KEYS TO SUCCESSFUL CHANGE

To Prepare for change:

- **Establish Urgency**
- **Clarity of Intention**
- **What is Your Why?**
- **Knowing**
- **Timeframe**
- **Honor Yourself**

Worksheet #1: "Getting Ready for Change"

Answer the following questions:

1. What are 3 things you can do to prepare for change?

2. What is your intention for this program? What do you intend to do or change so that you can nurture your heart and feel Optimized?

3. Why do you want to bring about this change? How will you benefit?

4. What unhealthy or negative thoughts or patterns of behavior will you need to abandon in order to change?

5. What is at stake if you don't change? How urgently do you need to begin?

6. Describe "where" you are now or how you are stuck and where you want to be when you finish all the activities this book.

7. What has to happen, how will you be different in order to know you have optimized?

8. When is your start date and by when will you have completed all the Activities?

9. What are 3 things you can do to honor and celebrate yourself as you have successes along the way?

> Insert your intention from Number 2 here for easy reference:

"You can have a big beautiful dream
and think about it often,
but if you don't make a decision to start
and pick a date
and follow a plan of action
with all your passion,
one day you will awake to
find yourself
older and
in the same place."
~Alletta Christenson Bayer

Positivity Pulse Points

- **Change is hard, especially as adults, but you have the power to change by taking intentional action.**

- It's imperative to engage both your thoughts and vision with your heart-felt passion. Bringing your whole self to the process will propel you forward.

- **Change is a process, and the key to successful change starts with preparing yourself, determining your why and your sense of urgency.**

- To make effective change, you need to know where you are starting from and where you want to end up. Journaling can be a helpful process to express yourself.

- **Timeframe is an important thing to determine before you start. Making a decision of when to begin and how long you will take to work through the process is an important part of your commitment.**

- Celebrate your successful implementation no matter how small or how big. Raising your positivity level by celebrating and honoring yourself encourages you to keep going, learning and practicing your new ways of being.

Journal for Clarity and Understanding

You might be familiar with the practice of journaling. Some people have a regular practice of recording and exploring their thoughts and experiences in a physical journal or in an online program.

Journaling is especially helpful if you are exploring new ideas, looking for clarity, or want to deepen your understanding. The idea is to get more in touch with your feelings and thoughts by taking the time to let them develop and flow.

There will be occasional journal pages throughout the Activities. They are for you. You can choose to share them or keep them private. You might even choose to keep a separate personal journal as you work through the program.

Here are a few helpful hints on how to journal:

- Find a quiet time and place where you are comfortable and select your favorite writing instruments or computer device. You may even want to have a dedicated notebook to write your private musings.

- Take some deep breaths in through your nose and out through your mouth and ponder the question or feelings you want to explore. Then write what you are thinking and feeling

- Allow yourself to tap into your intuition and creativity. Some people experience a deeper emotional connection to feelings when they write and others when they type.

Journaling provides you with an opportunity to explore and understand yourself better and to get clarity about things you may be feeling. You can create and write/draw anything you desire. If speaking works for you, then by all means dictate your thoughts and review them later. Go for it!

My Intention Journal

Using your new knowledge and intention, describe your ideal positive self, full of nurturing communications and energy. Paint or describe a colorful picture for yourself. Imagine scenes throughout your whole day. What old habits and ways of communicating would you like to release? What new habits and ways of communicating would bring you more joy throughout the day? Release your fears, judgments, and limitations as you imagine how things would change if you consistently received and delivered heartfelt positive recognition and appreciation.

Create an action plan. Do it. No procrastinating. Make it happen.

ACTION STEP 1: Determine and write at least one thing you could change about your belief by choosing to see what is strong and good about yourself/situation instead of what is wrong.

ACTION STEP 2: What is a negative thought or behavior you will commit to changing?

ACTION STEP 3: What is one step you can take TODAY to create change and begin to Optimize?

Check your pulse.
Self-Assessment: Time to OPTIMIZE

Answer the following questions:

1. What did you set out to do by starting this Activity?

2. What did you accomplish?

3. What do you need to change to be the person you want to be?

4. What is the Pearl of Positivity Wisdom you received this week?

5. What is your OPTIMIZE Action Step that as the CEO (CHANGE-EXCEL-OPTIMIZE) in your life you will commit to for this upcoming week?

"Replenishing your reservoir with loving,
social and emotional nutrients is an
investment in yourself.
We often forget to feed ourselves
with positivity and self-love
which results in feeling empty
and starved for the wrong kind of attention.
Intentions toward investing
in YOU will help grow your Inner Wealth™
and move you toward
abundance and prosperity
resulting in a rich relationship with
yourself and others."
~sherry blair

Optimize

ACTIVITY 2
Mindset:
Open to Experience Yourself and Others

One of the secrets of learning how to live more expansively is to open your eyes and heart to the positive inquiry of "what is strong" about a situation instead of negatively asking "what is wrong." Learning to look for what is going right in yourself, another person or situation involves sharpening your powers of observation. To help you do this we will introduce you to a number of characters. These characters will help you become more aware of different styles of relating and the effect those styles can have on self and others. As you read, you just might recognize yourself in one or more characters!

Activity 2 Objectives

- To open your awareness of the various positive and negative behavioral characteristics of daily communications with yourself and/or others

- To realize you have a habitual way of relating and communicating—and that you can add more positivity with conscious intention and action

- To understand the power and impact that your choice of thoughts, attitudes, words and tone has in your communication style

- To examine the current culture in your home and perhaps work "space" and the benefits of building positive human relationships whenever you encounter others

- To choose an intention to assist you in having clarity about the outcome you want from this journey

Activity 2 Summary

- Negative, fear-based, and sarcastic communication can be a default setting for many of us. Commonly, this sets up a negative environment and creates big problems later, such as unhealthy, perhaps volatile relationships, self-sabotage, anxiety, depression and loneliness. Those around you become discouraged because they are the recipients of negativity and in turn this creates even more negative behavioral choices and experiences. *It is a lose-lose situation.*

- *Appropriate* negative emotions such as grieving, anger at being abused, disappointment, fear of something that could harm us, etc., are useful and important to our well-being. To help you Optimize and Nurture yourself the goal is to reduce *inappropriate, unhealthy* or *gratuitous* negativity.

- All people develop best on a positive trajectory and flourish when they are regularly "fed" with detailed positive feedback. Make a point of acknowledging your *own* successes in detail, as well as those of others, even when those successes are small ones.

Take a moment to consider:

- Have you been a person who has had trouble experiencing healthy and fulfilling relationships?

- Are you on this journey to take your already positive relationships to a higher level of flourishing?

- Is there someone in your life who you feel is holding you down?

- Do you sometimes feel like you are getting nowhere?

- Are you zombie- like in life just pushing through to make it day to day?

There are many reasons that contribute to our unhappiness and negativity. Here are some:
- Worrying/Fearing
- Self-rating and rating of others
- "Awfulizing" things—Drama Kings/Queens
- Dogmatic Demands—Musts, absolutes, shoulds
- Inability to manage frustration
- Lack of personal boundaries
- Predicting the worst will happen
- Hopeless, stale thinking

Be More in Tune & Aware of Your Communication Style

First, let's introduce you to some caterpillars and butterflies that will help you determine your communication style. Yeah I know. Sounds a little weird, right? Just stay with us and use your imagination. But first we want to explain to you why we are using the concept of caterpillars and butterflies and how it relates to us human beings.

Why Caterpillars and Butterflies?

> "There is nothing in a caterpillar that tells us it's going to be a butterfly."
> —*Buckminster Fuller (1895-1983), inventor and architect*

Caterpillars need to find the right nourishment to eat in order to move through their early and middle stages into adult butterflies. If they do not get the right food, they won't make it or they will struggle to get there successfully. Using these characters as metaphors for human communication styles, we pretend the "right nourishment," positivity, is the food the caterpillars get that builds the foundation for them to optimize their full potential. Only then can they reach their full and glorious butterfly self. Feeding or being fed the "wrong stuff," or in other words negativity, is how they get off track.

Anyone who watches a caterpillar for any length of time knows that its main driving force in life is its appetite. It has an intense need to obtain as much nourishment as possible to prepare for transformation. Caterpillars eat constantly—and they can't eat just anything. Each breed of caterpillar needs a different kind of food in abundance in order to change and grow into a magnificent butterfly.

If you think about how this can relate to people, think about how different and unique we all are and all the different traditions that human beings celebrate. We all eat different cultural meals and have special family habits around meals. And each child, regardless of what choices of food she or he eats, grows into a beautiful person like the caterpillar grows into a magnificent butterfly. And there are many spectacular butterflies of all colors, shapes and sizes, just as with us people. We come in many beautiful shapes, sizes and colors from all around the world and with positivity, we learn how to embrace those differences and how to respect and honor each other as well as ourselves.

As with caterpillars, human beings require a huge amount of nourishment to grow and transform—but not just the caloric kind (most of us get too much of that). We thrive best when we receive abundant *spiritual and psychological* nourishment in the form of love and positive relationship. When we say love, we do not mean how you may feel about someone you like, as in a romantic way. We are talking about the nurturing type of love toward ourselves and others. We hunger for kind, compassionate and caring experiences. Our appetite for these kinds of positive relationships exist in all areas of life.

But if people experience too much negativity in their relationships and communications, it makes it more difficult to thrive and live life to their fullest potential. They may not recognize the greatness that is within themselves. The good news is by learning new habits of communication with self and others, they can lay down new habits and ways of thinking and begin to flourish, thrive and optimize. The latest research on brain plasticity shows us this is possible, and this book and exercises will help to bring about more positive transformation.

Back to the caterpillars...

In preparation for metamorphosis, the caterpillar weaves a silken chrysalis—a word derived from the Greek word for gold. It demonstrates that while change is inevitable, it doesn't have to be painful. For us humans, positive relationships help us grow in positive ways. They give us the hope, faith, and sense of self-worth we require to keep morphing into greater and greater versions of ourselves. And this is what makes a nurturing relationship really golden: people begin to see themselves as worthy, successful and genuinely want to build further success.

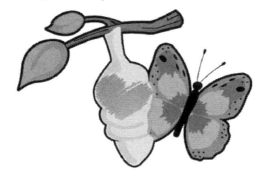

The caterpillar eventually and unquestioningly enters into transformation. Her body and her environment change in shocking ways as she follows her destiny. As she goes into the dark night of metamorphosis to emerge completely transformed, she exemplifies trust and hope—a model of transformation for those who feel held back from becoming their greatest selves by fear or uncertainty. The butterfly's transformation is a fitting symbol for the life journey of the human being. Hopefully, the twists, turns, setbacks, and successes we all experience contribute to morphing us into what symbolism writer Avia Venefica calls "ever-finer beings."

If we liken our human personal growth and transformation as caterpillar-selves transforming into butterfly-selves we realize that our qualities of greatness are in us all along. That butterfly-ness is in our DNA just as butterfly-ness is in the DNA of the caterpillar. The metamorphosis is just about optimizing the expression of what we have always possessed.

PLEASE NOTE: The following exercise is by far the longest in the whole program, but it is the MOST IMPORTANT.

EXERCISE 1: Open to Experiencing Yourself and Others in Your Life

See if you can recognize or identify some of your own personal characteristics in the characters below. Imagine that these characters' roles are applicable in any setting at home, work and play.

Let's explore the qualities of the individual caterpillar characters. The gender is interchangeable for each character.

EXERCISE: If you feel you possess some of the characteristics of each caterpillar, put a number in the blank from 0 to 5, 0 meaning you don't feel you have any of the characteristics, and 5 meaning you have a high degree of similarity.

0	1	2	3	4	5
Not At all like me		Somewhat like me			A Lot Like Me

_____ **"Fragile Franny"** is the one whose feelings we are commonly afraid of hurting and we walk on egg shells around her. She is ultra-sensitive and can pout or turn on the tears whenever she senses criticism or doesn't get her way. But truth be told, Franny uses these strategies to manipulate or control others in order to get her way.

_____ **"Bleeding Heart Helena"** feels sorry for everyone and often puts her needs last. She seems self-sacrificing and co-dependent all the way to the finish line, but often begins to resent putting herself out for others and not feeling cared for in return.

_____ **"Nervous Nellie"** can't sit still for a moment. She is constantly on the go and her nervousness puts everyone on edge. She is just a bundle of nervous energy and high anxiety.

_____ **"Obsessive Al: AKA Anal AL"** strives for perfection. Can't get a darn thing done because he obsesses over being perfect. He doesn't want to put his work out there unless it's perfect, but since he never feels it's good enough, his projects just continue to pile up.

_____ **"Sarcastic Sam"** speaks mostly with a sarcastic tone. He claims he's just joking but typically it's really a passive aggressive style that is meant to hurt others.

_____ Living life is a joy for **Isabella**. She seems to be smiling from the inside out and anyone can tell she is flourishing. She feels supported and appreciated. She relies on her inner positivity to continue growing and changing in a positive way. Whether she is with family, friends or at work, she understands her value and practices self-appreciation. Occasionally she makes mistakes, after all, no one is perfect. There is no fallout and no drama. She doesn't waste time dwelling on what went wrong. Instead, she tries to learn from her mistakes and quickly steps back into the greatness of who she is.

_____ When **Justice** makes the effort to do well, he goes through his day at a snail's pace. He often is plagued with a great deal of negative self-talk frequently allowing WMDs (Worry, Misery and Doubt) to get in his way. At the end of each day, he feels as though he's had nothing but junk food to eat—he constantly seems to crave much more. He never quite feels satiated and often feels lonely. Justice sometimes just seems to be going through the motions at home and at work. At work, he becomes fearful that he won't meet his deadlines or that he may not survive a round of layoffs, should that happen. Sometimes Justice wonders why he even bothers to come to work. He works just as hard as Isabella and his accomplishments are similar to hers, but for some reason she is usually happy and seems to be changing and growing—even transforming. It also seems that she is more liked than Justice. "It's just not fair," Justice grumbles.

Isabella notices that Justice gets very stuck. Justice is brilliant and can be very funny. Unfortunately, he has not learned yet how to make the best choices and he is commonly eating a lot of junk food in the form of negative self-talk. He allows himself to be plagued with worrying, misery and doubtfulness.

In all fairness to Justice he is dealing with a lot at home. Life can be difficult sometimes and it is not easy to navigate life's stressors. The amazing thing about Justice though is that he has so many great things about him but he often cannot see them. Sometimes he just won't let anyone help and that is a big mistake. He gets off track a lot.

Not only does Justice literally feed himself junk food in the form of negative self-talk, he also makes unhealthy food choices and doesn't exercise. His pulse is clearly flat-lining.

The Three Opponents to Inner Peace: WMDs

(Worry, Misery & Doubt = Weapons of Mass Destruction)

Justice gets himself bogged down with negative thinking and not-so- smart choice making. On top of dealing with all his life stressors, he constantly battles three internal major opponents:

Worrying William, Miserable Marvin and Doubting David. He has yet to learn how to shake off their negativity.

_____ **"Worrying William"** worries about practically everything which ultimately leads him into a state of anxiety. When Justice fuels the thoughts that come from this part of his brain he starts his entire day worrying before he even gets out of bed in the morning. He has not learned to ask himself, "How is worrying about this or that going to help me? Is my worrying going to change anything? Will worrying solve my problems? How is worrying preventing me from achieving my work goals? How is worrying affecting my stomach? Does worrying about my wife and children make things any different?" If Justice were willing to open his mind to get help with this, he would learn how to counteract these irrational thoughts and his anxiety would be reduced if not eliminated.

Although it is healthy to have some nervous feelings about things in life, such as deadlines at work or school, and to be concerned about things in life, too much worrying leads to anxiety and sometimes causes lots of stress to build up inside our bodies. (NOTE: In the OPTIMIZE: 7 Steps to Healthy Rational Thinking, we delve into this deeper.)

_____ **"Miserable Marvin"** is moody and for the most part in a state of depression. He refuses to talk to anyone about it or get help. He makes poor choices like sometimes using alcohol and smoking weed to feel better. He claims he is a social drug user but truth be told he is using drugs to change his mood. When he is in a really bad mood, he can be very mean to others around him. He may bully, tease or be sarcastic especially if he is feeling lonely or down on himself. He may procrastinate or miss important deadlines or isolate himself from others, which only serve to make him feel more depressed.

When Justice has gotten himself buried in misery by listening to Miserable Marvin, he can get in a lot of trouble. He even wonders to himself, "Why am I being this way?" or "Why am I doing these things?" But he just cannot seem to shake it. Justice is not proud of this and privately admits he has been emotionally abusive to himself and others in his past and at times falls back into that trap.

Justice has a right to be sad or angry just like anyone else. These are natural feelings. Sometimes he gets disappointed, which is another healthy negative emotion, but it quickly spirals into unhealthy depression when he is listening to Miserable Marvin. When he gets angry he often flies into a rage and spirals out of control. Instead of talking about how he is feeling, he often makes reactive, self-destructive and impulsive choices.

_____ **"Doubting David"** rates himself and others in a very negative way. He puts himself down and starts to believe he is not good enough. He begins to get off track at home and work, often isolating himself from his family, friends and co-workers. When Justice identifies with this part of his brain, he rates himself and others in a very negative way.

Imagination time. Do you identify with these characters in your leadership positions at home or work? If yes, in what way? Be honest—even if it is a little bit. Write your answer below:

Mr. Moody, Mrs. Crabtree, and Mr. Silencio, exemplify leaders who are stuck in a unique way. Each encounters different kinds of obstacles to imparting their wisdom and greatness to the people in their lives. These leaders have diverse qualities and strengths. Their management styles are well established, but if they could only learn some skills to get "unstuck" they would be much more effective leaders. If you identify with any of their characteristics in your leadership roles at home, work or play, put a number from 0 to 5 in the blanks.

0	1	2	3	4	5
Not At all like me			Somewhat like me		A Lot Like Me

_____ **"Mr. Moody"** is a seasoned leader. He has contributed in magnificent ways. Although he regularly thanks others for doing a good job, his moods can sometimes make him difficult to get along with. He himself has tons of management experience, but for some reason he seems stuck—he has not moved far enough into his own potential to set a truly inspiring example for others.

_____ **"Mrs. Crabtree"** is task oriented and full of wisdom. But in her role as a leader, she seems to spend much of the day barking orders and punishing others. She has a tendency to lecture when someone does something wrong. Even on a good day, she's abrupt and a bit crabby; she's in a constant state of frustration because she only sees mistakes all around her! She can't seem to be consistent in her disciplinary actions enough to have a positive impact. At the same time, she doesn't ever seem to notice when others are shining.

"That's just what I expect from them," she'd likely say if someone asked her why she never gives positive feedback to anyone. "They're going to have to do a lot better than that to get a pat on the back from me! Besides, they're just doing what they are supposed to be doing!"

In private moments, Mrs. Crabtree feels unhappy that she can't seem to get others to perform better. She means well, but wonders why she doesn't feel as if she is flourishing at home or work or reaching her full potential. Like Mr. Moody, she knows that she isn't setting a great example for her fellow leaders or for the family members who count on her for guidance—but she doesn't know how to change to set this example.

_____ **Mr. Silencio** is the quiet type, but his contributions to the team are nothing less than stellar. He has studied lots of management theory and prides himself on understanding employees, but he has trouble implementing what he has learned for their benefit or expressing himself to them or his family.

Although frontline workers, fellow team members and even family members learn a great deal from his intellect, he says barely a word to them directly. Whether they're doing well (which gives him a good feeling) or breaking the rules (which bothers him), he says nothing. People have no trouble getting away with rule breaking when he is around. On the other hand, they don't feel inspired to do a better job, because Mr. Silencio doesn't seem to have a preference or a voice one way or the other. He is stuck in his own thoughts.

Mr. Kodak, Mrs. Polaroid and Ms. Canon believe that creating nurturing relationships and an environment where everyone thrives is all about celebrating what's going well—their focus is on what's strong NOT wrong!

They do not agree with top-down autocratic, self-righteous styles, choosing instead to value the voice of every single person around them. Their mission is to nurture personal growth and development—to support everyone in their transformation to greatness. Their transformation into effective leaders is complete, and they're ready to show others the way.

One of their "secrets" of staying so upbeat personally positive is that each one makes a practice of always nourishing themselves for what is going right and their good decisions and choices. This practice helps them appreciate their own strengths and continue to grow as a person, a leader and a compassionate friend. And when they do make mistakes, they don't dwell on them. They learn from their decisions and think about how they could do things differently next time.

_____ **Mr. Kodak** seems to notice everything that's going right. Whomever he speaks to goes away feeling special. Even if it's something small—a choice to follow the rules, or just showing up and paying attention—he has something good to say about it. Practically everywhere he goes, Mr. Kodak takes "snapshots" of successes, both miniscule and massive, and he's unfailingly generous when giving feedback to his family, friends and co-workers about those successes.

_____ A bit more seasoned, **Mrs. Polaroid** can keep up with Mr. Kodak in terms of noticing and acknowledging success. Like a Polaroid camera, she captures successes as they happen, then deepens that image of success by clearly stating how those successes reveal people's strengths and virtues. Her unique, intense style of relentlessly recognizing others takes some getting used to, but in the end, this ability to hone in on what's going right—and on what's so right about it—makes her an invaluable role model for leading the positivity process and helping everyone grow.

_____ **Ms. Canon** is the ultimate policy implementer and relentless rule follower, but she's not one to lecture, reprimand, or scold when rules are broken. Instead, she recognizes rule following. She helps to keep everyone on track at work or home by offering frequent reminders to those staying on task: "You are wonderful for not breaking rules and for upholding our values." Ms. Canon appreciates everyone for their willingness to change old habits, for staying in healthy control and for re-routing themselves back on track when they break rules or fail to comply with rules and guidelines for living a rational, positive, healthy and loving life. She's firm and strict, but also compassionate, loving, and proactive.

Senora Corazon, CEO

(Change—Excel—OPTIMIZE)

_____ **Senora Corazon** has been accused of wearing rose-colored glasses. She seems to believe, sometimes almost beyond reason that all people can flourish. Her view is that giving recognition for every success, brilliance, and accomplishment is good for everyone, including the one who gives that recognition. She loves to notice what others are doing in the moment—or even what they're wearing!—and to take time to tell them what she's observing. She communicates to everyone around her that she values them for their positive attitude and efforts to make the world a better place.

Even when those around her seem to be having a rough day, she finds ways to positively acknowledge them for their ability to deal with hard times or difficult tasks. Senora Corazon is especially magnificent at bringing others into balance when necessary.

While she doesn't always hit the mark herself, she responds to her own errors and negative thoughts by redirecting her focus to what's great and right in the moment. Senora Corazon has blossomed into a brilliant leader—the most brilliant of them all.

Worksheet #2: "How Do I Experience Myself?"

Answer the following questions:

1. Which "caterpillar character(s)" do you currently identify most with and why?

2. What words describe your thoughts or feelings after reading about the characters?

3. While reading about the characters, which of your communication "habits" came to mind?

4. Which character would you choose to be more like and why?

5. Has learning about these characters impacted the way you see, think, and/or feel about positive versus negative communications and attitudes in your life?

6. In your life, do you tend to look for the positive and the greatness in people and situations? Or do you tend to look for what is wrong or complain about it? Do you ignore what is wrong, or blame others or judge them negatively? Explain and give some examples:

Review: Set an Intention for Yourself

- It is important to know what you want before you can take action to make it happen. Otherwise, without knowing clearly what you want, you can't determine the first step to getting started.

- Intention is one of the most powerful forces in life you can harness. Without a clear intention, you can wander around without meaning or direction. But once you find clarity of intention, you can set your stake in the ground and chart a clear course around it, and all the forces in the universe will seem to align to make even the most impossible possible.

- Sometimes in the early stage of imagining what you want you might have only a vague idea or desire. If you desire clarity but are having a difficult time figuring out what that is—don't worry. This is the time to dream and to imagine different possibilities. You might even feel you can't find a solid idea or a direction to latch onto. Some people describe it as a feeling of swimming around in a deep pot of soup. This "swimming in the soup" can actually be very useful. In fact, some people find they must spend time in this stage of imagining while they are trying to find clarity or while they are exploring different options. But be aware that a pattern of remaining vague after evidence or options are weighed can sabotage your forward motion of change, leading to confusion, inertia, and stagnation. A pattern of vagueness or indecision may even be an attempt to control the situation by not setting a clear intention or taking action. This can keep the status quo or cause others to make decisions for you, setting up an unhealthy dynamic which either of you might come to resent.

- An intention can be long-term or short-term. It can be something for everyday or even every moment. It can be about something in particular or about a quality in life or a way of being. It could be something as simple as deciding to write down 3 things that went well for you each day, or it could be longer term such as deciding to change your career by a certain date. Whatever your intention might be, it is important to state it so that you can focus your attention, take action, and measure your success.

- When you set and state an intention, you are making it clear to yourself and others what you want to do.

Worksheet #3: "Positivity and Intention"

Answer the following questions:

1. On a scale of 1 to 10, 10 being the most positive and joyous daily experiences you can imagine, what number do you give to the amount of positivity in your typical daily life right now?

2. Using the above scale, what number do you give yourself as the person who creates or contributes to these positive and joyous experiences?

3. If you rated the positivity in your life less than 10, what effect do you feel that has on your morale and satisfaction with things in your life overall?

4. And what about your feelings of well-being? Internally—in your heart, mind and body.

5. If you increased your overall positivity significantly, how might that impact the way you relate to yourself?

6. Do your interactions with others get you the results you want? What typically happens?

Worksheet #3: "Positivity and Intention"
Continued

7. If you were to experience more positivity in your relationships with others, what benefits do you think or feel you would gain?

8. What benefits might others gain if your relationships had more positive interactions?

9. Where do you want to be when you come to the end of this program? In other words, what is your intention for yourself? For example: I intend to communicate more effectively or I intend to feel more positively connected to people or I intend to deliver heartfelt recognition and appreciation to myself at least 5 times a day. Write your intention here:

10. What would you have to do, change, or give up to make your intention possible?

11. What are some of the benefits you would receive as a result of living your intention?

Insert your intention from Number 9 here for easy reference:

What is your action plan to make your intention come to life?

My Positivity Journal

Using your new knowledge and intention, describe your ideal positive self, full of nurturing communications and energy. Paint or describe a colorful picture for yourself. Imagine scenes throughout your whole day. What old habits and ways of communicating would you like to release? What new habits and ways of communicating would bring you more joy throughout the day? Release your fears, judgments, and limitations as you imagine how things would change if you consistently received and delivered heartfelt positive recognition and appreciation.

Create an action plan. Do it. No procrastinating. Make it happen.

ACTION STEP 1: Determine and write at least one thing you could change your attitude about by choosing to see what is strong and good about yourself/another person/situation instead of what is wrong.

ACTION STEP 2: Choose two to three people with whom you interact at home, work or in your recreational life and focus on giving them some positive recognition this week. Write their names here and what is strong about them that you choose to recognize.

ACTION STEP 3: What is one step you can take TODAY to create change and make your Positivity Pulse begin?

Check your pulse.
Self-Assessment: Time to OPTIMIZE

Answer the following questions:

1. What did you set out to do by starting this Activity?

2. What did you accomplish?

3. What do you need to change to be the person you want to be?

4. What is the Pearl of Positivity Wisdom you received this week?

5. What is your OPTIMIZE Action Step that as the CEO (CHANGE-EXCEL-OPTIMIZE) in your life you will commit to for this upcoming week?

*"The effects of positivity are not random.
They are predictable and sweeping.
Your life is a complex tapestry of
your psychological strengths,
mental habits, social connections,
physical health, and more.*

*In the span of three months,
positivity can change these
various parts of you
in beautiful synchrony.*

*At a deep level,
positivity can change
who you are.
And those changes can
make life itself more fulfilling."*

~ Barbara Fredrickson

Optimize

ACTIVITY 3
Build:
Nurtured Heart® Foundations

Enjoying a flourishing life with a strong positivity pulse is all about having compassion for yourself, nurturing your own heart and cultivating positive relationships. Activity 2 has opened your awareness to different styles of relating and how positivity and negativity in relationships impact us.

In Activity 3, you will discover four key concepts that are the foundation for building a Positivity Pulse in yourself and your relationships. As you read the stories let yourself think about how you can transfer your understanding to situations in your life. Doing the exercises will help you build your skills.

Activity 3 Objectives

- **Learn the Four Foundational Concepts that support the Nurtured Heart Approach®**

- **Understand how to apply the concepts in relationships**

Activity 3 Summary

- **Become aware of when you "light up" and where or how you give your energy**

- **Remember Baby Stepping to create personal success and success in those around you.**

- **The Toll Taker teaches that you get to choose how you interpret things.**

- **Game Theory explains why clear rules and clear consequences are important.**

> "If we commit to harnessing the power of games
> for real happiness and real change,
> then a better reality is more than possible—it is likely.
> And in that case, our future together will be quite extraordinary."
>
> ~ Jane McGonical, *Reality is Broken: Why Games Make Us Better and
> How They Can Change the World*

The Four Foundational Concepts

Foundational Concept I

We are the toys. Think about the famous toy store "Toys R Us."

We learn at a very young age how to create relationships and get attention. In fact, we are born with the power to learn how to conduct ourselves based on the responses we get from others. Parents, caregivers, teachers and other adults are like children's "favorite toys." No other toy can match what these people can do. They express countless emotions, expressions and energies in response to children's behaviors, especially negative behaviors.

Children watch carefully from infancy to see what their favorite toys do in response to their choices, both good and bad. Adults "light up" with sounds and actions in response to these behaviors, in effect teaching children how to get what they want or how to get the attention they crave, even if it's negative attention. If children can't get adults to pay attention to them when they are behaving well, they will misbehave in order to get attention. Children quickly and easily learn which behaviors get them the most energetic attention, and those are the behaviors that will be repeated. This is how children learn to behave in the world, because children crave attention.

There is a pretty funny YouTube video called, "**Why waste a temper tantrum if nobody is around to see it?**" If you can, watch it now. This little toddler shows great self-control. When his mother is not in the room, he immediately stops his tantrum. He then searches for her, and the second he finds her, he immediately throws himself back in temper tantrum behavior. He is lighting up with negative behavior, but his parents are not responding to it. He likely wants something he cannot have and was told the word "no." His savvy parents have learned how to deal with his tantrums – Don't give them any attention.

As adults, we continue to make choices in our thoughts and behaviors based on the responses we get from others. What do you normally do when you are told "no" or can't do or have something that you want?

Be honest. Do you sulk and pout, or scream and yell to get what you want?_____

As social beings, we continue to require love and attention from friends, co-workers, and family members. Sometimes we make stories more dramatic, or we may even flat out lie to get attention, to make friends, or to make people laugh. In fact, it is pretty safe to say that almost everyone has done this at least once in his or her lifetime. In more serious situations, some of us act out violently either physically or with abusive language.

Name a time when you made up a story or gave it more drama to make someone laugh, to make a friend or perhaps to get out of trouble:

What was the outcome? How did the person respond to your story?

On other occasions, have you ever wanted to hurt someone because that person hurt you? (not physically but with words)

Were you successful? Did your action create an angry or sad response from that person?

In these instances you were lit up like an exciting toy. The other people were lit up as well but all related to negative experiences.

To build a strong Nurtured Heart® foundation, learn to turn your energy "upside down"

DON'T:
- Feed negative energy or drama by lighting up or responding to negative behaviors from others.

- Act out your own negative thoughts.

DO:

- Turn your positive energy "on" and light up when you are being successful or see others being successful.

- Take action to handle negative thoughts or behaviors in a healthy and safe way.

It is natural to seek feedback and reinforcement from others in the form of energy and attention. In this way, you can think of yourself as a "toy" from which you want to get and give as many positively energized relationships as possible.

You can find and practice ways to see and verbally acknowledge success—or energize success for your good choices and thus increase your positivity and your confidence in your ability to make good choices. And when you do this for others, you will be nurturing their success and building positive relationships with them.

KEYS TO SUCCESSFUL CHANGE

Find ways to give positive energy, response, and relationship for the good stuff, just like Senora Corazon and the Nurtured Heart® Warriors Team.

My "Favorite Toy" Journal

Write about a current or past relationship in your life. On a scale of 1 to 10, 10 being the most "lit up," how easy was it for you to get their "bells and whistles" going? Did their reactions to your successes and/or mistakes encourage you to do your best? Describe how their reactions or lack thereof made you feel and what effect their reactions had on your desire to do your best.

Foundational Concept II

Baby Steps: Catching Yourself Being Good vs. Creating Being Great

Imagine a baby getting ready to take the first step of her life. What a precious milestone parents eagerly anticipate and celebrate as their little baby does what comes naturally. What drives her to want to leave the warm safety of her bed or her parents' loving arms to rock, roll, and crawl and eventually to walk and run? Where does her desire and drive come from? It's innate. Her greatness is within her, expanding from birth in every cell of her body from her brain to her toes. Her muscles grow as she kicks and rolls, her brain develops, her desire to walk upright like others she sees pushes her forward. There are no conscious thoughts of fear or failure holding her back. And, unless she has a disability, nothing can stop her from growing and expressing her greatness.

From becoming strong enough to roll over, to sitting up by herself, to crawling, to pulling herself up and walking around a low table holding on hand by hand, wobbly step by step – she keeps exploring and learning new feats. And then plop! She falls down, only to get up and practice again. And what do we do? Do we wait until we catch her walking before we acknowledge her accomplishments? Do we reprimand her for falling down? Do we ignore her progress until she can run to us when we call her name? No! **We marvel at the miracle of every new step. We clap and verbally express our delight with enthusiastic energy. We acknowledge and encourage each tiny movement in the desired direction.** We celebrate with her and anyone who will listen that our baby took her first steps. We have a mindset to support our growing baby's healthy development. And our enthusiastic and positive encouragement becomes a vital part of egging her onward to greater successes.

If we are nurturing parents, we apply this intention of positively supporting and encouraging each small baby step that our children take as they grow and learn and make choices in their lives.

As adults we can nurture ourselves by employing this same positive mindset for the "baby steps" constantly happening within us. We can learn to look at ourselves with the eyes of a loving parent and appreciate the difficulty of change and growth we are experiencing. We can commit to see, acknowledge and support the baby steps happening whenever we are learning new habits or skills. We can express our delight in any number of ways to celebrate each and every little "movement" or success along the way.

This concept speaks to the importance of energizing, rewarding, and celebrating success every step of the way with yourself and others. It speaks to the importance of finding ways to create success instead of "catching" it. For example, if you decide to only acknowledge yourself after a big success and not to acknowledge yourself for your small successful steps along the way, you'll miss infinite opportunities to nurture, appreciate and motivate yourself throughout each day. And if you bring negative energy whenever you fail to soar to great heights of achievement—as Mrs. Crabtree does by reading the riot act and carrying on when things go wrong—you'll set up an environment of negativity, making it more difficult to sustain your motivation and work toward success. The Nurtured Heart Approach® teaches tools for seeing and acknowledging success in yourself and others, no matter what. Every time you take a baby step—no matter how small—success is created.

> "Having a commitment
> to a purposeful life means
> that you want to have a
> positive impact on the world and others.
> This reveals other qualities of your greatness.
> It shows that you have a vision beyond
> any self-serving lifestyle.
> You care about the world and
> the feelings and well-being of others.
> This alone conveys that you are thoughtful
> and considerate and that
> you want to see the best in people.
> These are incontrovertible reflections
> of your loving and caring nature,
> discipline, wisdom, and good judgment."
> ~Howard Glasser

Worksheet #4: "Baby Steps"

Answer the following questions:

With the concepts of Catching Success and Goodness vs. Creating Being Great, reflect on a key relationship you've had and how it inspired you to do your best, or not, and how it affected you emotionally. It should be one of the most intense relationships you've had, whether positive, neutral, or negative. Recall aspects of this relationship that affected your feelings of yourself, your confidence, and the quality of your relationship with that person.

1. Did you look forward to being around that person again?

2. Did you feel "seen" and valued for your efforts?

3. What kind of feedback did you receive?

4. Were you encouraged or challenged to use your key strengths? In what way?

5. Did you feel your "voice," opinions, or suggestions mattered? Why or why not?

6. Did you feel your contributions mattered? In what way?

7. Was it a supportive relationship or competitive and isolating? Explain:

8. Did you feel appreciated?

KEYS TO SUCCESSFUL CHANGE

Reinforce and energize yourself and others:
- For following rules
- For showing good judgment
- For living values like:

empathy	conscientiousness
thoughtfulness	responsibility
respectfulness	punctuality
resourcefulness	decisiveness
competence	conscientiousness
creativity	generosity
caring	reliability
tolerance	determination
hard work	compassionate

Worksheet #5: "A Key Relationship Experience"

Answer the following questions, reflecting on what you wrote in "My Favorite Toy" and "Baby Steps" Worksheet pages:

1. Reflecting back to your key relationship, was there a single aspect of that relationship that stands out in your memory? Describe.

2. Knowing the "Favorite Toy" concept, and reflecting back on that relationship, are you aware of any action you took, or didn't take, to get attention from the person with whom you were relating?

3. Did you feel reinforced and energized when you had even small successes? In what way?

4. Were your larger successes recognized and celebrated? In what way?

5. Again reflecting on your journaling and your new understanding, what additional kinds of attention could you have benefited from?

The Nurtured Heart Approach® teaches us to take every opportunity to create successes that would otherwise not exist. If we find ways to honor ourselves and others for what isn't wrong, we have a whole lot more to celebrate.

But wait! Celebrate what's not going wrong? Create success that would otherwise not exist?

How does one do this without being a total Pollyanna, pink-washing the world until everything looks rosy and ignoring problems?

Consider the tale of the Toll Taker, the next foundational principle of the Nurtured Heart Approach®.

Foundational Concept III

Toll Taker: Choosing the Way We See Things

In his presentations and books, Howard Glasser shares an old story about a dancing Toll Taker on the San Francisco Bay Bridge. The professor who originally told Glasser this story reported that he had driven over to the dancer's lane to pay his toll. "It looks like you're having the time of your life," the professor told the Toll Taker. The Toll Taker replied, "Of course! I have the best job in the world and the best office in the world." He colorfully describes the beautiful views he drinks in daily. He gets to see sunrises and sunsets while on the job—and, as luck would have it, he's an aspiring dancer who gets paid to practice in his glass-walled office high above the water! When the professor inquiries about the other Toll Takers who don't seem so energized, the dancing Toll Taker responds, "Oh, those guys in the stand-up coffins? They're no fun!"

We get to choose how we see things. The Toll Taker could have focused on the difficult aspects of his job: long days on his feet, car exhaust fumes, or disgruntled commuters. That's what the guys in the stand-up coffins are likely focusing on. He chooses, instead, to dwell on what's right about where he is and what he's doing. The best part about this story is that it teaches us that we get to make the choice of what we focus on or how we see things in any given moment of the day. No matter how much we've dwelled on the negative in the past, each new moment is an opportunity to see and acknowledge what's right in our worlds and in those people around us.

You get to choose how *you* perceive things.
And *you* get to choose how *you* react.

Choosing to focus on what's right is about getting negative thoughts and emotions out of the way so you can see what's strong and positive about a situation. Focusing on the positive allows you the space to broaden and expand your understanding. Open your mind and open your heart. This allows you to view the situation from a higher perspective. You can have the freedom to discover the lessons that could be learned from the situation. From this place you can use your heart and mind to "think outside the box" like the Toll Taker. You can bring your creativity to imagine several possibilities to solve the problem. By focusing on what is going right, instead of being stuck wallowing in negativity, you can open yourself up to positive choices. And with positive choices you can set your intentions to climb to ever greater heights of success.

KEYS TO SUCCESSFUL CHANGE

In an instant, we can decide to see what's going strong, thereby changing our experience of the moment.

Worksheet #6: "I Choose the Way I See Things"

What Do I Focus On In a Negative Way?	I Can Instead Choose to See What Is Strong About This Situation

The Evidence is in...

Just in case you might still be wondering why you should add a healthy dose of heartfelt positivity to your daily diet, below is a sampling of the scientific evidence (Fredrickson, 2009) that has been pouring in over the last few years linking positivity and health. (NOTE: In the OPTIMIZE series for positive psychology, we provide more research and ways to deepen your experiences in love and positive emotion.)

People's increased positivity predicts:

- **Lower levels of stress-related hormones**
- **Higher levels of growth-related hormones**
- **Higher levels of bonding-related hormones**
- **Higher level of dopamine**
- **Higher levels of opioids**
- **Enhanced immune system functioning**
- **Diminished inflammatory responses to stress**
- **Lower blood pressure**
- **Less pain**
- **Fewer colds**
- **Enhanced sleep**
- **Less likelihood of hypertension, diabetes, or a stroke**
- **Longer, healthier lives**

Foundational Concept IV

Game Theory: Clear Rules, Clear Consequences and Right Back in the Game of Greatness!

Think back to the characters from Activity 2. We typically respond in various ways when rules are broken or when we are off track with goal attainment. Although there are nuances to the variations, we either over-react like Mrs. Crabtree, don't say a word and avoid like Mr. Silencio or indiscriminately respond based on our mood like Mr. Moody. Over time, our typical way of responding becomes habitual, but with awareness and intention, we can learn to respond in more positive and productive ways, thus changing our relationship with yourself and others.

Think about how easily we can speak of our failures or flaws. We can come up with a bunch of excuses or put ourselves down when we get off track in reaching our goals. Similarly, we treat others in our lives the same way—some more critically than others. When we fail to strictly and clearly delineate and enforce rules, or uphold our values related to our personal code of conduct, we enable and allow rule breaking and the pushing of boundaries around rules. This is a surefire recipe for negativity as some of us dance around the rules to see how far we can push them. This isn't because we are ill intentioned or bad people; it's just the natural pull of that uncertainty as to where the boundaries and limits really are.

We are "leaking" negative energy when we break rules, make poor decisions, veer off track because we can, or when we are not motivated to live in alignment with our values. It's up to us to refuse to give energy and attention to that negative behavior and to instead choose, consistently and firmly, to create positive acknowledgment and connection around successful behavior and positive relationships. Each decision we make throughout each day either gets us closer to our goals for personal success and positive relationships or leads us farther away. If we put our attention on acknowledging and celebrating our positive behaviors we will move faster toward the person we want to be.

In the Nurtured Heart Approach® the answer is to hold up video games (or pinball games for those of us who were born too early to have gotten on the video game bandwagon) as a model for effective rule making and enforcement. These games are designed to offer **_continuous positive reinforcement_** in the form of points, sounds, and visuals for as long as the player is successful.

Research shows us one reason why these games are so compelling is that the continuous positive reinforcement of these games stimulates the area of the brain concerned with rewards and pleasure, making it enticing to play for hours on end (Welsh, 2011). When a rule is broken or the player loses the game, the positive reinforcement stops...but all it takes to get back in the game is a simple reset, and the whole thing with all its accompanying pleasure starts all over again. No adverse consequences, no punishment, no penalty—just an unceremonious reset to get back in the game.

Think about your favorite sport. How are the rules enforced? In response to a foul, an immediate penalty is imposed, but then the game continues. In response to a broken rule or a lost point, the referee generally blows a whistle, calls it what it is, and enforces the penalty, then gets the players right back in the game.

So, with this idea in mind, how might you react to someone being negative toward you? Or toward yourself for falling off track with your diet or exercise plan? In the Nurtured Heart Approach®, the response to a broken rule, or falling off track is a simple, un-energized reset or timeout, just like those in the video games or sports and a warmhearted welcome back to success as soon as rule-breaking stops. If you make a poor decision, acknowledge it, and reset yourself to get back on track. When you handle things in this manner you avoid shaming yourself or someone else. This technique will be described in much greater detail later on.

So you see, game theory in the NHA is about clearly enforcing rules without energizing rule breaking, and about encouraging rule compliance by energizing that compliance **while it is happening.**

KEYS TO SUCCESSFUL CHANGE

Choose to clearly define rules and to consistently refuse to energize the breaking of rules (or the pushing of boundaries around rules).

When disciplinary action is necessary, give them in an un-energized fashion. All energized response comes when rules are not being broken.

This, together with the intention to energize success, is the NHA's default setting. We energize and create success and refuse to energize negativity.

Worksheet #7: *"Be Self-Aware of Negativity Triggers"*

Write some examples of things that cause you to react with negativity either about something you fail to achieve or get off track with or as it relates to someone else. You know, those times when someone breaks a rule or does something to really make you want to lose your temper. Writing down your usual way of reacting will help you pinpoint areas where you need to practice enforcing rules without energizing rule breaking.

What happened? What is the event?	How Do I React?	What can I do differently?

Positivity Pulse Points

- **We learn early on how to get relationship—both positive and negative. For many reasons, we have been inadvertently conditioned to focus more on our shortcomings and sweep our success under the carpet. Begin to nourish yourself and others with all the emotional nutrients required for positive growth and change and you will flourish in synchrony together.**

- Positive recognitions are energizing in a way which support and encourage the recipient to feel more connection with the giver. Your self-recognition has the same effect resulting in a desire to continue striving toward greater heights of happiness and satisfaction.

- **Negativity, even toward yourself, saps energy and holds you back from achieving goals and experiencing a healthier self-relationship. When you are negative toward others, it can also encourage the recipient to seek attention by making more negative choices.**

- Negativity toward other people saps their energy and can affect their ability to achieve their goals and to build healthy relationships with themselves as well as others. It can also encourage the recipient to develop the bad habit of seeking attention by making more negative choices.

- **We can languish or just give a minimum effort when we are deprived of positive social, emotional, intellectual and for some, spiritual relationships.**

- To feel emotionally connected to others is a basic human need. The stronger the positive relationship connections one has, the more that person will flourish. Individually, our Inner Wealth® and experiences of self-love and unconditional self-acceptance are built through positive interactions with self and others.

- **Having a voice, feeling appreciated, valued, and connected are the real key factors that inspire us to create happiness and greatness in our lives.**

Create an action plan. Do it. No procrastinating. Make it happen.

ACTION STEP 1: Identify one person in your life who you allow to push your buttons and get your attention with negative behavior. Resolve to take action at least once each day this week and say something positive to them before they have a chance to act out. To whom and what will you say?

ACTION STEP 2: Identify one person in your life that needs guidance in doing a task. Remember Baby Steps and set the bar for them as low as possible so that they can experience success and you can acknowledge it. For whom and how will you set the bar low for them?

ACTION STEP 3: Identify at least one rule or a value that is not upheld in your life that often gets pushed to the limits. Notice and write down whether or not the rule, or personal code of conducted is stated unclearly.

Check your pulse.
Self-Assessment: Time to OPTIMIZE

Answer the following questions:

1. What did you set out to do by starting this Activity?

2. What did you accomplish?

3. What do you need to change to be the person you want to be?

4. What is the Pearl of Positivity Wisdom you received this week?

5. What is your OPTIMIZE Action Step that as the CEO (CHANGE-EXCEL-OPTIMIZE) in your life you will commit to for this upcoming week?

"By discovering,
appreciating and
developing
your own greatness,
you are able to
share it with the world."
~Alletta Christenson Bayer

Optimize

Optimize

ACTIVITY 4
Support:
Three Stands™ that Support the Methods

In Activity 3 you discovered the four key concepts that are the foundation for building a Positivity Pulse in your relationships. Here in Activity 4 you'll learn the Three Stands™ that support the method. You can think of them like a tripod, each supporting the other, together strong—equally important.

While you may be anxious to jump ahead to the next Activities, it is important to build your understanding of the method because each layer is necessary for you to be able to successfully implement the approach so that it becomes your own "default method" of relating. These Three Stands™—or commandments—provide clarity and are the underpinnings for the methods you will learn in the next two Activities.

Activity 4 Objectives

- Learn the Three Stands™ that will give you clear direction and resolve.

- Establish values and rules to live by.

Activity 4 Summary

- **Stand One**: Absolutely NO! I will not energize negativity.

- **Stand Two**: Absolutely YES! I will relentlessly energize and nurture greatness in myself and in others.

- **Stand Three**: I refuse to let it slide when I cross the line into negativity, I will actively remember to reset, and to use the energy of negativity as an impetus to go further into greatness.

The Three Stands™: Clear-Cut Commandments

The Three Stands™ are the support system of this approach. Any time you aren't sure how to act or react to a situation, checking back in with the Three Stands™ will give you direction and resolve. (The recognition strategies described in the next sessions are the "how" to implement the approach, and all work to uphold these stands.)

> ## STAND ONE
> ## Absolutely NO! I will not energize negativity.

Not sure what a "negativity leak" might look like? It's happening any time:

- You lose your cool when a rule has been broken or put yourself down for getting off track.
-
- Problems or issues captivate and elicit your charged response.
- You expect someone to do something wrong so you can reprimand him.
- You are willing to focus energy and attention on poor choices.
- People in your life are able to "push your buttons" by making poor choices or breaking rules.

When you have a "negativity leak" you give relationship in the form of recognition. Energy flows more strongly as a result of the person doing something less than acceptable—leading that person to perceive, on a deep, subconscious level, that more recognition and attention is available in response to wrong behavior.

KEYS TO SUCCESSFUL CHANGE

Stand One is about *not undermining* the effectiveness of the approach by "leaking" negativity. It is important to realize that everybody leaks negative energy sometimes. Luckily, this approach does not require perfect execution in order to effect massive change. We're all human and we all make mistakes and leak negative energy at times. It's how we rebound from that mistake or leakage that makes the difference. As soon as you notice a leak, you can change course and step cleanly into a new moment of positivity.

Worksheet #8:
"Places Where I Leak Negativity"

Okay, it's time to "fess up." Even if you resolve to practice these stands as if your life depends on it, you're only human, and even you will leak at times. In order to help you become more aware of where or when or with whom you need to be on your best guard, be proactive and make a list right now. Be sure and also use examples. Use yourself in the examples since you're working self-nurturing. Give specific examples.

EXAMPLE: I tend to lose my temper or patience with _____ when they _____ _____.

EXAMPLE: When the _____ rule is broken, I tend to lecture (myself or another) on and on about _____.

1.

2.

3.

4.

5.

> **STAND TWO**
> **Absolutely YES! I will relentlessly energize and nurture greatness in myself and in others.**

Remember Baby Steps? Set the expectation as low as you can in order to catch, create, and celebrate successful moments. And don't forget the Toll Taker with his positive message—you get to choose how you see things—whether you decide to see what's strong or what's wrong. The decision is up to you. Once that resolution is made, you can use the techniques for creating and energizing success and positivity that are covered in the next two Activities.

By choosing to notice and energize what's right, we show people that their favorite toy "does lots of cool stuff" when they are successful, and that the toy get boring when rules are broken, boundaries are pushed, or they fail to show up as the great beings they are.

And you can be your own "favorite toy" by giving yourself lots of nurturing appreciation and celebrating when you have successes large or small!

SUCCESS STORY

There are so many stories I could share regarding relentlessly and strategically drawing myself into a new and renewed way of living. I have accomplished great strides in the 4 years since I learned about NHA and have had many life changing revelations and experiences.

What I have decided to share is that NHA is not a one-time strategy to learn and arrive at your destination of greatness. Rather, NHA is a daily decision to wake up, look into your heart and see yourself for who you truly are and the greatness you possess regardless of your circumstances.

The story that stands out most in my heart is how I was trying to prove to my therapist that I was broken beyond repair and that while I could understand NHA and how it applied to my life moving forward there was nothing really that could repair the past. I came with a demonstration to her of with two vases – one whole, one shattered. I told her that I wanted to be like the whole one and have value and worth. Instead I was the broken one and no longer served a purpose. Upon hearing this, she pulled up a website where beautiful art was made from broken glass and asked me if the artwork I was seeing had no value. The irrefutable evidence was in front of me as I looked at the artwork and could not deny the exquisite detail and value that each piece of art had. It was from here that I launched into discovering my worth from a different perspective. While I saw myself as broken, it was the incidents in my life that were really what made me the strong resilient person I was and am.

I carried around the pieces of broken glass in a jar for quite some time as I was not quite ready to let go of what was represented by those pieces of glass—the hurt, resentment, brokenness. However, about 8 months later I was able to sit in my therapist's office and empty the jar and begin to let go what was holding me back.

I have been able to share this story with many struggling with worth and guide them along on their pursuit to wholeness. You see, greatness is a daily practice. Looking at life through the eyes of your heart versus the eyes of your head changes perspective and directs you to your true inner self. It is a journey, not a destination and it is on this journey that true worth is discovered.

Laurie Lee

Character Strengths, Values, and Virtues

In their book Character Strengths and Virtues the late Christopher Peterson and positive psychology pioneer Martin Seligman expand on the notions of character, values, and virtues by creating and defining six categories of human strengths that are valued across cultures:

- Strengths of wisdom and knowledge—creativity, curiosity, open-mindedness, love of learning, perspective

- Strengths of courage—bravery, persistence, integrity, vitality

- Strengths of humanity—love, kindness, social intelligence

- Strengths of justice—citizenship, fairness, leadership

- Strengths of temperance—forgiveness, mercy, humility, modesty, prudence, self- regulation (self-control)

- Strengths of transcendence—appreciation of beauty and excellence, gratitude, hope, humor, spirituality (Peterson and Seligman, 2004)

Consider how the values that are important to you might fall into these categories. On any given day, you can choose which category you would like most to acknowledge in your life. Have fun and do strengths dates or family activities.

> **"To cultivate the greatness within you, seek daily opportunities to nurture your character strengths and values. Acknowledge your growth and celebrate your successes to blossom into the best version of yourself."**
> **~Alletta & Sherry**

Worksheet #9: "My Personal Values"

Are any of the above categories of character strengths and virtues explicitly valued in your life? Do you know your values? If so, list them below. If not, which ones do you feel could be important to your life to strive for?

List the values individually or group into categories:

With the notes you made above, decide upon or state your values in phrases or sentences so that you anchor them deeply.

Worksheet #10: "Celebrate Success"

One terrific way to nurture success is to have ways to energize and celebrate your success and the success of others when they least expect it. A little extra effort on your part goes a long way to make them feel seen, valued, and appreciated. Brainstorm and list some ways that you can celebrate, appreciate or recognize your success. Then, list some ways that you could celebrate others in a meaningful manner that might surprise them. For example you could send them a nice email or leave them a personal recognition on a brightly colored Post-It® note.

1.

2.

3.

4.

5.

Firmly Establish Your Values Before You Set the Rules or Develop your Personal Code of Conduct (Your Commandments)

Oops! Maybe you're anxious to jump right in and learn how to enforce your rules in your home, or construct your personal code of conduct for living life, but forgot to establish your values first. Do not move forward to set or enforce established rules, or a personal code of conduct until you establish your values first. This is because values have to be identified before rules are created. Here's why: when you acknowledge that each chosen value represents a strongly held belief, you intuitively understand why a corresponding rule is established. The rules are there to support your values. After you determine your values, then the rules or your personal code of conduct make much more sense. "Here are the rules I choose to live by because I need to have ways to uphold my values." See how much easier it is to live in alignment with your values versus, "Here are rules I must follow because they are good rules." Adherence to the values is what creates your personal buy-in for your rules/personal code of conduct and drives decisions for your behavior. Then, your decisions will be based on upholding your values and any need to "reset" stems from not living in alignment or getting off track with your values.

What a positive difference stated values make—they help define what is important to you. So if you haven't yet defined your values, or they don't correspond to your rules/personal code of conduct, now is a great time to figure those out.

For example, if these are your values:

- I honor and respect myself and others.
- I treat myself and others with dignity and respect.
- I care about myself and every person in my life and commit to being kind and compassionate.

Then three obvious rules that could come from these values would be:

- No passive-aggressive statements. No sarcasm. No negative self-talk.
- No gossiping. No disrespecting others.
- No teasing or being mean.

Below are some more examples of personal values:

- I commit to creating peace within my heart and toward those around me.

- I communicate openly and move toward harmonious solutions.

- I am aware that oppression exists and believe in equal treatment regardless of race, gender, Sexual orientation, religion, age, or cultural ethnicity.

- I have integrity and uphold honesty in my life.

When you identify and understand your values it makes for a much more meaningful way of establishing rules/personal code of conduct for yourself in any environment. And when you use recognitions to notice values sincerely, they serve to accelerate living with integrity and spiral positive feelings.

> "Achievement of your happiness
> is the only moral purpose of your life,
> and that happiness,
> not pain or mindless self-indulgence,
> is the proof of your moral integrity,
> since it is the proof and
> the result of your loyalty
> to the achievement of your values."
>
> Ayn Rand

> **STAND THREE**
> **ABSOLUTELY CLEAR!**
> I refuse to let it slide when I cross the line into negativity, I will actively remember to reset, and to use the energy of negativity as an impetus to go further into greatness.

This stand is about knowing the rules and your personal code of conduct cold, about reinforcing and encouraging yourself and others in your life for not breaking them, and about being absolutely consistent about giving a consequence whenever rules are broken. This is tricky when you are doing this with other adults. Think in terms that the consequence is about you taking a stand for what you believe in as opposed to a traditional consequence. Consider that when someone pushes your buttons, that you will calmly respond in a way that allows for effective communication and peaceful conflict resolution. When a rule is being broken by children (if you have them), reset them back to their greatness, welcome him or her back "into the game" and move right on to the next moment of success. Don't leak energy to the problem of a broken rule—on the contrary, problems get no emotional play. No backlash, no long-term repercussions. Just a reset and then an openhearted invitation back to the greatness that was always there.

A Word About Using Resets

By now you might be wondering how you can enforce the rules. You start by withdrawing energetic connection. Enforce a broken rule with as little energy, emotion, and drama as possible. Remember Mrs. Crabtree who gives long lectures. She demonstrates that her energy was most accessible in response to the breaking of a rule. In this way, some children or adults realize an intense connection is most possible when negative things occur. This is often how others get our attention - with negative behavior.

To avoid this dynamic, refuse to give your precious energy to problems. In Activity 7, you will learn about using a "reset" as an immediate consequence of breaking a rule. You will learn to take a stand to enforce the rules.

BUT FIRST - you need to learn the energizing methods in the next two chapters . Before you start using resets it's VERY IMPORTANT to deepen your relationship with yourself or others with the positive recognitions you will be learning in the next two Activities to begin to shift any negative dynamics that are creating your personal or interpersonal turmoil.

State Rules in the Negative

Begin to manifest Stand Three by stating rules in the negative. This makes "in-bounds" and "out-of-bounds" absolutely clear. Remember the Game Theory concept. If the rules are not stated in the negative, then where is the line of non-compliance? By not having them stated in the negative, there is too much room for pushing the limits. With clarity comes better understanding for all. For example:

- NO allowing disrespect
- NO being late for work or appointments
- NO spreading the infection of a negativity
- NO sarcastic comments
- NO racist, sexist, homophobic, ageist, or religious jokes or comments
- NO cheating on my diet

Worksheet #11: "Rules"

If you do NOT know your rules, or personal code of conduct, it's time to get busy. If you already have written rules, check to see that they are written in the negative, as in the examples above, and reword as necessary.

Looking back to the worksheet, "My Values," write your new rules, stated in the negative, that correspond to your stated values.

For example, the values statement: We treat each other with respect.

The rule might be: No yelling. No sarcasm. No cursing when we communicate.

1.

2.

3.

4.

5.

Positivity Pulse Points

- **Refuse to give energy to negativity.**

- Resolve to energize success no matter what—even if you or someone else is just doing what is supposed to be done.

- **Shared values are important to creating shared culture. From the values, rules will logically follow.**

- Resolve to have clear rules, stated in the negative where possible.

- **Adhere to the three stands with unwavering conviction and the energy in your life will quickly shift.**

Create an action plan. Do it. No procrastinating. Make it happen.

ACTION STEP 1: Be mindful of your own thoughts as you go through each day. When does negative self-talk come up? (If none—congratulations!)

ACTION STEP 2: Is there a particular person you seem to have the most negative interactions with at home or at work? Notice the circumstances that seem to initiate negativity. Use the concepts you are learning to try and decipher if the person is looking for more connection with you. Write what you notice.

ACTION STEP 3: Resolve to nurture success this week. Spread your positive comments around to others in your life at home, work and play. Each day, say at least one positive comment more than you would ordinarily say to each person. Jot down to whom, what you said, and their reaction.

Check your pulse.
Self-Assessment: Time to OPTIMIZE

Answer the following questions:

1. What did you set out to do by starting this Activity?

2. What did you accomplish?

3. What do you need to change to be the person you want to be?

4. What is the Pearl of Positivity Wisdom you received this week?

5. What is your OPTIMIZE Action Step that as the CEO (CHANGE-EXCEL-OPTIMIZE) in your life you will commit to for this upcoming week?

"Learning the
Nurtured Heart Approach®
to get a Positivity Pulse is like learning
a new language,
and like any new language,
it takes practice and perseverance.
It demands that we stop leaking
our own negativity while holding
a mindset that is governed by
open-mindedness and
open- heartedness."

~ sherry blair

Optimize

Optimize

ACTIVITY 5
Discover:
Strategies to Support the Stands

Your awareness of communication habits has been opened, you understand the Foundational Concepts, and you have learned the Three Stands™ that support the methods of growing positivity and flourishing in your life. In this Activity, you will learn the first two recognitions that help you create an upward spiral of positivity.

Apply these strategies daily, like your life depends on it. Apply them to yourself in your self-recognition practice. Sprinkle them around on everyone you come into contact with and you'll beam heart energy all day long—and so will those you recognize!

Activity 5 Objectives

- **Discover Active Recognitions and how to use them for self-recognition and to make others feel seen, valued, and appreciated.**

- **Discover Experiential Recognitions and how to use them to reinforce and increase your Inner Wealth® as well as making investments in the well-being of others.**

- **Become more aware of greatness happening all around you and how to celebrate it.**

- **Learn how to address negativity and non-compliance and reset back to greatness.**

Activity 5 Summary

- **Active Recognitions: a verbal snapshot of what you or someone else is doing when he or she is acting positively and making wise choices.**

- **Experiential Recognitions: expanding on an Active Recognition by adding a description of values being reflected in your positive choices, behaviors, and decisions as well as those you see in others.**

- **Values and character strengths can be appreciated, amplified, and strengthened by using recognitions.**

- **Resets are used to redirect self and others from negativity back to positivity.**

Strategy 1: Active Recognitions

- Active Recognitions are so simple to do that at first you might feel they are insignificant. But don't be fooled! They are so profound because they can notch up the positive energy between two people, within a family, with friends, or even at work very quickly.

- Most importantly, because change starts within, it best to start the practice of actively recognizing yourself.

- An Active Recognition is simply giving a verbal snapshot of what you see when a person is acting positively. You are not giving any kind of judgment. For example, "Aliyah, I notice you're here on time for our workout session."

> ## How to Give an Active Recognition
>
> Step 1. Clearly observe what you or the other person is doing when acting in a positive manner.
>
> Step 2. Offer a "verbal snapshot" of what you see, avoiding any kind of judgment. When applying to yourself, reflect on what you are doing—or say it aloud! Tell someone!
>
> • The most useful words for giving Active Recognitions are "I notice" and "I see."
>
> • Stay in the here and now.
>
> • Do NOT lecture, preach, or leak negative energy about how "it's better than last time…"
>
> • Use this technique throughout the day toward yourself and others at home, work and play as often as you can.

Even if you or someone in your life is just doing what they are supposed to be doing, consider all the ways in which she's being successful and making choices that are positive. Most of us aren't accustomed to acknowledging ourselves or others for the little things done right. We have often heard people ask, "Why should I acknowledge anyone for doing what they are supposed to do?" The reason why is that you want to change the energy of the individual relationships and the culture at large. You want to notch up the Positivity Pulse in your relationships—and it starts with you giving positive energy to yourself, to everyone you can, one person at a time. The positivity jolt people get from giving or receiving positive recognition feels so good that in no time at all, you will notice the domino effect starting to happen as others begin to do the same thing – to give recognitions in their circles of influence, and so the positivity spirals upward!

Active Recognition Examples:

"Michael, you just got very angry with me, and you stayed calm."

To yourself: "I am doing great at multitasking today! I'm working toward my goal of staying organized."

"I notice I am staying on my diet and making healthy choices."

"Drew, I noticed you helped out that man who seemed lost."

"Today I worked out and followed my exercise plan."

"Toni Anne, it's clear to me you are so excited to learn new things."

"Shana, I notice you brighten the whole office with your big smiles and positive energy."

Optimize — Take a moment to OPTIMIZE yourself now. What do you notice about yourself right now in this moment that is positive, constructive, and/or productive? Write it down. If you have more than one, go for it.

KEYS TO SUCCESSFUL CHANGE

HOW TO GIVE ACTIVE RECOGNITIONS

By relaying the picture exactly as we see it and calling out the positive attributes being demonstrated, the person feels seen, acknowledged, and appreciated. When applied to yourself, you are self-recognizing your accomplishments, helping you stay on track and motivated.

Use Active Recognitions:

- Only for positive moments (remember the Toll Taker: that if you choose, you can see positivity almost anywhere). Be aware that positive moments are also those moments when you are handling yourself with grace and dignity and respect toward others even when you are angry or frustrated.

- Never in reference to rule-breaking or negative behavior.

- By employing neutral, non-judgmental language to make the message as "digestible" as possible.

- With as much specificity and details as possible.

With these simple recognitions, you are laying the foundation that will allow you to take the approach deeper with added texture and more heart-felt compassion as you move into using the next three techniques, all of which build on the first one. With each recognition, you are helping yourself or another person feel appreciated or seen in a new way. When applying it to yourself, you are changing your story, increasing your own positive emotion, and rewiring old negative thoughts. Repeated recognitions, especially as you go deeper into the approach, build what we call **Inner Wealth**™, which means you or the person, starts to "own" those positive qualities you are calling to attention.

Worksheet #12: "Using Active Recognitions"

Reference the guide below, and then write your own examples. Use Active Recognitions to:

• Recognize yourself for your wise choices.

• Prove that no one is "invisible." State that you value someone for who he or she is in that moment.

• See and celebrate yourself and others.

• Invite conversations that can lead to respectful and peaceful exchanges.

• Enhance positive regard and conversations around culture and diversity.

EXAMPLE: "Honey, thank you for making the bed before you left. I really appreciate it."

1.

2.

3.

4.

5.

Worksheet #13: "Practicing Active Recognitions"

It feels great to be the recipient of positive recognitions. It also feels great to give them. If at first you feel awkward, GREAT! That just means you are stretching a little and learning a new way of relating. It will become easier and easier—and pretty soon it will become automatic! It is especially useful for those of you who see the glass half full, or may be more cynical and negative than most.

Using the table on the next page helps you break down the different stages of interaction to make you aware of both sides of the interaction—the *POSITIVITY PULSE*.

ASSIGNMENT: At least three times in the morning and three times in the afternoon*, give an Active Recognition and note it on the table below. This includes virtual recognizing in emails, texts, instant messages, Instagram, etc.

HINT: Print out pages to keep handy for use each day this week or email optimize@sherryblairinstitute.com for free handouts that you can save and print.

* Extra points for practicing and noting more than six times per day!

Worksheet #13: "Practicing Active Recognitions"

What You Saw or Noticed	What You Said	Recipient's Response	How You Felt

(Note: Email optimize@sherryblairinsitute.com for the free downloadable worksheets and self-assessments.)

Strategy 2: Experiential Recognitions

With this technique, you build on Active Recognitions by adding a description of values being reflected in your positive choices and what you see in others. With this strategy, recognize yourself (or another) in the moment of living desirable values and demonstrating strengths. In this way, you continue to build Inner Wealth® and reinforce character strengths, values, and virtues.

When you use this type of recognition, you are amplifying Active Recognitions by including a positive judgment and/or value attached to the statement. Give recognitions and appreciations that are specific, detailed, and based on observable positive behavior.

Positive values are behaviors or thoughts deemed by society as intrinsically good or worthy of imitating. A list of values and strengths you might want to acknowledge and strengthen might include:

Adaptability	Altruism	Caring	Compassion	Commitment
Confidence	Cooperation	Courage	Creativity	Cultural sensitivity
Determination	Enthusiasm	Expressive	Fairness	Good sportsmanship
Hardworking	Helpfulness	Honesty	Humility	Inner strength
Integrity	Inventive	Kindness	Leadership	Loyalty
Open-hearted	Open-minded	Patience	Peaceful	Professional
Resolve	Resourceful	Respect	Responsible	Self-control
Self-motivated	Team player	Thoughtful	Tolerance	Wisdom

Or using statements such as:

Using good judgment   Using good manners   Being a positive role model

Motivated to grow and learn

Optimize — What can you add on? What is something you see about yourself in this moment?

How to Give an Experiential Recognition

Step 1. Start with an Active Recognition

- (Clearly observe what is happening in the moment or what you or someone else is doing as it relates to positive emotional and behavioral choices.

- Try starting with "I see..." or "I notice..."

Step 2. Add a comment that reflects a value or strength.

- Apply this technique when you are upholding your personal code of conduct or notice others following the rules and upholding values.

- Be genuine and show excitement (in your own way). Don't be insincere or overly exaggerated.

- Remember Baby Steps and the Toll Taker. To create success, change your view of the situation by looking for the positive aspects.

- Use this technique throughout the day toward anyone in your life and yourself, as often as you can.

Example to the person making your morning coffee: "I appreciate that you remember what I get every morning and get it started when you see me. You are so quick and have a great memory."

A DAUGHTER'S SELF-CARE SUCCESS STORY

About three years ago, my teen-age daughter leaned over to me while we were sitting in church, and whispered, "Mom, I want you to know I've committed to eating Gluten-free." I was surprised to hear this resolution. Whether it was something the pastor said that inspired her or some other inspiration, I didn't know. But I acknowledged her choice with as much positivity as I could while trying not to disturb the people around us. I was also grateful, as she had been struggling with health issues in the last couple of years since she had started eating foods containing gluten again.

Diagnosed as a baby with Gluten Intolerance, she rarely intentionally ate gluten until Middle School. She wanted to eat what all the other kids were eating. You know teens want to fit in and will push the limits! Probably what finally influenced her the most regarding her choice were the black and white numbers she saw on her blood test results and the acknowledgment of her physical symptoms.

Regardless, I was grateful but took a wait and see attitude. During the ensuing years I've used Active Recognition and Experiential Recognition every day to encourage her good choices and to help her build Inner Wealth®. Every day. Her conviction has been strong from that first day, and I feel my active support and positive recognitions have reinforced her commitment. She asks about ingredients when she eats away from home, and reads labels so she can live in integrity with her choice.

I am so proud of my daughter's continuing success with her resolution to be gluten-free and enjoy good health. We are both so happy to see her health improving. And I am so thankful that these simple tools of recognition helped me help her build Inner Wealth® and better health!

Alletta Bayer

Remember Mrs. Polaroid, who flows gracefully in her ability to experientially recognize the people with whom she comes into contact daily? As a more seasoned Nurtured Heart® warrior, she has the ability to use positive judgments and value statements to develop and deepen characteristic strengths and virtues. She does it in her own unique, intense style—and you can too.

Experiential Recognition is a right-in-the-moment opportunity to anchor in the values, philosophy, and rules in your life at home, work and play. This is how to move beyond the "thank you" or "great job" you may have been using conventionally. Here you have the golden opportunity to further enforce and uphold the values in your personal life, within your family, with your friends or in your workspace on a daily basis.

Experiential Recognition Examples:

"Last week I worked out three days on the elliptical machine for thirty minutes. Today I added an extra day and increased my time to 35 minutes. I'm really advancing and showing my commitment to achieving my forty-five minute workouts five days a week!"

"It was really difficult to pass up that chocolate birthday cake last night, but I showed real willpower and did it. Must have whacked 500 calories off my plate right there! Yea for me! I'm sticking to my plan of NO desserts and I feel terrific!"

"Camille, I see you're working through that page of difficult word problems. That shows you have great perseverance even in the face of such a challenge."

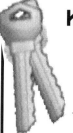

KEYS TO SUCCESSFUL CHANGE

Focus on recognizing qualities and strengths you want to see grow in yourself and others around you.

Give recognitions early and often—daily! Don't be selfish—do it with strangers, with family, friends and co-workers.

Don't be discouraged if you are met with resistance.

Remember Stand Two
Resolve to purposefully create and nurture success and greatness. Be relentless.

Worksheet #14: "My Top Three Character Strengths"

A. Gather your thoughts and note what you believe to be your top three character strengths. (Or ask others around you—family members, friends, co-workers to reflect back to you what they see as your top strengths.)

B. Give a short example of how/when those strengths are evident:

C. How or in what ways could you use this strength more often?

1. Strength:

A. Who identified this strength?

B. How/when is this strength evident?

C. How/in what ways could I use this strength more often?

2. Strength:

A. Who identified this strength?

B. How/when is this strength evident?

C. How/in what ways could I use this strength more often?

3. Strength:

A. Who identified this strength?

B. How/when is this strength evident?

Worksheet #14: "My Top Three Character Strengths" Continued

D. Use your new tool of Experiential Recognition to write an Experiential Recognition for each strength you listed.

Identified Strength 1:

Experiential Recognition:

Identified Strength 2:

Experiential Recognition:

Identified Strength 3:

Experiential Recognition:

Try this activity with your family, friends or co-workers. Name the people now that you want to "test" this out on:

What was the experience like? What happened? Write it down and anchor in the positive emotion.

"You've got to take an active role
not only in noticing your
strengths, but by identifying
what they are—
out loud or in writing.
By taking this action,
you are anchoring in
positive emotion
and in turn,
this becomes your essence."
~sherry blair

Positivity Pulse Points

- **As soon as you begin your journey of applying the recognitions to yourself and others in your life, you begin to embrace and elicit the Positivity Pulse you are nurturing.**

- When even small details are positively noticed and recognized out loud (or through written communication), or through self-recognition, the recipient feels irrefutably noticed, acknowledged, and appreciated for doing what she or he is supposed to be doing—working, being responsible, following rules, and showing positivity.

- **Using recognitions instead of the usual perfunctory salutations proves to the people in your life that they are not invisible—they are "seen" and celebrated each time they walk through the door.**

- No matter what, everyone has a right to be acknowledged and treated with dignity, respect, and integrity. Everyone deserves proper emotional nourishment and feedback for contributions to the Positivity Pulse in your life. Everyone deserves to be energetically nourished for his or her role in your life.

- **By using Active and Experiential Recognitions, you are seeing, naming, and appreciating the greatness you see in yourself and in people all around you.**

- Notice and honor people's differences, uniqueness and diversity. Use recognitions to encourage conversations for deeper appreciation and understanding of what brings us all together but also what makes us unique and beautiful in our differences.

Create an action plan. Do it. No procrastinating. Make it happen.

ACTION STEP 1: Make a list of your own qualities, strengths, and values you admire and/or want to expand. Copy them on a paper or index card you can post where you can see it, or put them in your phone, calendar or other electronic device so you can keep them handy. Each day choose one to focus on. Actively seek evidence of it in your activities, and then recognize yourself.

ACTION STEP 2: Pull together a "Positivity Tribe." Consider people from all parts of your life: at home with family, in your friendship and community circles and at work. Resolve to recognize each other with Active and/or Experiential Recognitions at least 10 times each day. (Even if you were to say several sentences for 15 seconds for each recognition that is only a total of two and a half minutes!) This approach doesn't take much of your time throughout the day. Just become aware of what people are doing and energize them with a few sentences at a time. If you practice daily, it will become a habit! List some ideas to get you started:

ACTION STEP 3: Find people that you do not ordinarily interact with on a daily basis—perhaps someone you work with and barely spend time with—a family member with whom you have lost contact—a friend that you miss. Make it your habit to recognize and appreciate them on a daily basis. List some people and qualities/strengths they have or things they do to get you started:

Check your pulse.
Self-Assessment: Time to OPTIMIZE

Answer the following questions:

1. What did you set out to do by starting this Activity?

2. What did you accomplish?

3. What do you need to change to be the person you want to be?

4. What is the Pearl of Positivity Wisdom you received this week?

5. What is your OPTIMIZE Action Step that as the CEO (CHANGE-EXCEL-OPTIMIZE) in your life you will commit to for this upcoming week?

"Your most valuable resources
in life are your very own
positive strengths,
character traits
and virtues.
Let them shine
and you will become
who you were meant to be."

~Alletta Christenson Bayer

Optimize

Optimize

ACTIVITY 6
Accelerate:
Strategies to Spiral Positivity

You already have great tools to consistently recognize and notice positivity flourishing in yourself and all around you. And with daily practice you will create even more positive energy for yourself and others to enjoy.

In this Activity, you'll learn how to creatively promote commitment to your personal code of conduct or commandments for living and for upholding values and rules in your family, with friends and even in your workspace. You'll learn in a deeper way how to create successes that would not otherwise exist.

Activity 6 Objectives

- Discover what Proactive Recognitions are and how to accelerate your commitment to your own personal goals or code of conduct as well as with the rules and boundaries you have in your family, at work and elsewhere.

- Learn what Creative Recognitions are and how to confidently use them to create abundant success and positivity for everyone.

Activity 6 Summary

- By focusing on and appreciating positive accomplishments instead of dwelling on what is not done, you energize yourself and each person's desire to achieve greatness.

- When you are being supportive toward your own well-being as well as caring about others, you can all thrive creatively, intellectually, emotionally, and socially, and that benefits everyone.

Strategy 3: Proactive Recognitions

Proactive Recognitions build on both Active and Experiential Recognitions, but with an important twist: we notice and verbally acknowledge moments when we or someone in our lives is ***not*** breaking rules or living out of alignment with their values.

Whaaaatttttt?! This might sound absurd at first but ultimately this technique can be incredibly energizing! Intentional celebrations of moments where problems are not occurring give you vast opportunities for positive reflections. Rather than giving energy to yourself or another person only when a rule is being broken or there's a threat of it being broken, this technique gives energy in response to rules not broken. The person comes to see that much positive attention is available in return for following the rules and living their values. You get to notice that you did not go off your diet, or spend money needlessly, or choose not to exercise, etc. Giving a Proactive Recognition is much easier than it may sound. Read on to learn how and you'll be a pro before long!

Proactive Recognitions inspire you to comply with rules by creating more internal positive messaging about what you *could* be doing in terms of violating your own contract with yourself. They accelerate and deepen the refusal to energize negativity, moving you into a new realm of success. They help you counteract the tendency to create energized connections in your brain and in every cell of your body around the temptation to break the rules or act out of alignment with your values. It's a great way to tap into heart-centered proactivity and to gently re-direct yourself away from negative reactivity.

Establish Values First Before Rules

You'll need to do this step before you can be a pro at using Proactive Recognitions. Let's review the Values to Rules Positivity Pulse concept from Activity 4. Be sure you established and have a very clear understanding of what your values are in all aspects of your life. You need to determine and understand your values before you create your rules or personal code of conduct, because they are intimately connected. When you understand each of your values, you will intuitively know what the negatively stated rule is that upholds each value.

We're not talking about a long list of rules, but rather a few choice rules to live by. If "rules" sounds a bit too much for you, you could create a personal code of conduct (or name it something else) that exemplifies your values. The concept here is that if you don't have a list of values that are meaningful to you and which you try to live in alignment with, then you won't have any guidance about how to live your life. Values and rules, as we'll call them, gives you a direction and guidance for your behavior. Adherence to your values is what creates your buy-in and commitment for living in alignment with your rules and drives your decisions for making positive choices day by day in your life. This concept holds true whether you are determining your own values and personal code of conduct or whether you are doing so with your family, at work or other community in which you are involved. Your decisions and actions are based on upholding the values and "resets," which help you stay on track and which you'll learn about in Activity 7, stem from being out of alignment with your values.

For example: If you value a healthy environment, one of your rules might be "No Smoking." Not only would you personally be committed to not smoking, but you would have a rule of No Smoking in your home or car or other such place as you have control over. When you value a healthy environment, not only do you not want to poison yourself by smoking, you also don't want to breathe second-hand smoke nor have anyone else that you care about breathe those toxic chemicals either. Living in alignment with your value of a healthy environment demands your compliance with your rule of No Smoking. And if someone enters your space who doesn't share this value and breaks your rule, then you would "reset" them by informing them of the rule and asking them to comply. We'll talk about resets in the next Activity.

State Rules in the Negative

Proactive Recognitions begin with your understanding and desire to live by your values. If you didn't review or write your rules in Activity 4, go back and do it now. Take a deep dive into your core being, pull the energy between your heart and mind and begin by completely embracing what you believe is your personal code of conduct—your commandments for how you want to live your life. Make sure the rules stem naturally from your values and are stated precisely and negatively (starting with the word "No...") when possible. Rules may require modification to fit these parameters. If this is the case, then get to it!

Once those rules have been established or re-established, they need to be clearly and strictly upheld by you in order to get what you want in your life. Here are several examples of personal code of conduct rules:

- **No being an "on demand channel" anytime someone texts, emails, messages or calls.**
- **No doing to others what I would not do to myself.**
- **No ignoring my need for self-care—healthy eating, exercising, friendship and family time, sleep, hobbies, etc.**
- **No gossiping about other people**
- **No allowing myself to be disrespected or disrespecting others.**

How to Give a Proactive Recognition:

- First, identify values and define corresponding rules as negative rules that start with the word "No."

- Then, be on the lookout for the values being upheld and the rules followed, and make a point of recognizing yourself and others for following the rules and upholding the associated value— especially for those times when you or those around you have a tendency to break particular rules repeatedly.

- Talk about rules in the context of them being followed rather than only bringing them up when someone isn't following them.

Reflect on the Toll Taker and Baby Steps. Choose to see the rules that are followed and the smallest possible movement to create success. Move away from reacting to rule breaking and into Proactive Recognition of rules followed and values upheld.

Proactive Recognition Examples:

"Wow! I feel really great and I'm proud of myself for not staying up past my weekend bedtime! I could have chosen to go out after the party, but I'm committed to get my 8 hours of sleep every night. I made a great decision and voting for my own well-being. Yay me!"

"Hey Mike, I noticed you didn't grab the ice cream when you went to the fridge. Way to go! You made a healthy decision to eat the veggies instead. I can see you are really committed to your healthy eating plan. I admire your perseverance!"'"

"Hey Margaret, I noticed you weren't late to our work-out session. That shows me you're committed to yourself and to me for getting our full session in. I really appreciate you helping both of us stay on track."

"What does it hurt to point out to yourself that despite your fantasy of throwing something out your window in a fit of road rage, you're continuing to follow the rules?

This serves you in two ways:

first, by giving you a chance to acknowledge to yourself your angry impulses; and second, by giving you a chance to shift that energy into a much more constructive course of action—recognizing yourself for your power of restraint, discernment, wisdom, kindness and healthy control as you choose to behave in accordance with your values despite temptations to do otherwise."
~Howard Glasser

Strategy 4: Creative Recognition

Create Successes that Would Not Otherwise Exist

Creative Recognition builds on Active Recognition, using clear, simple commands and bigger-than-ordinary positive acknowledgements in response to even small gradations of compliance.

Remember Baby Steps: recognize and celebrate each small step forward and encourage forward movement to the next step and you will see each step builds upon itself. Eventually the small successes lead to larger successes and to the change you want to accomplish.

Creative Recognition is a way of making those steps available and rewarding for even your most challenging situation or even a difficult person in your life. This strategy makes success unavoidable— and retrains you to ensure that you are self-recognizing and shining plenty of energized positive connections even in response to the smallest success.

How to Give a Creative Recognition to Yourself

- Observe yourself and when you are about to do exactly what you are supposed to do, such as leave the house on time, sit down and pay the bills, choose healthy foods at the market, go to your exercise class, etc.,

- Make a request to yourself with which you're already on your way to complying. Voila! You've created a moment of success.

- As silly as it sounds, you will be building positivity and reinforcing your good choices. Try it and see how good you feel by giving yourself heartfelt recognition!

For example:

Let's say you've decided to make healthy food choices, and you have made a rule of "No junk food." Imagine you are at a friend's party and on your way to the table of food. As you're heading in that direction, say something like: "I need to go right to the healthy choices." Then as you bypass the junk food and opt for the veggies use a Creative Recognition and say to yourself: "What commitment I just showed to myself! I just chose to pass right by the junk food. That shows my determination! I'm choosing to support my healthy goals and make healthy food choices – even at a party. I can choose success! Yay me!"

If you have a bad habit of interrupting people but you value connection, you could make a new rule for yourself of "No interrupting." Then the next time you find yourself with others, observe yourself. When you are about to burst with something to say, instead say to yourself: "I can feel I am just about to burst with something to say, but I need to listen attentively, focus on what he is saying, and wait until he is finished." Then when you have successfully done so, tell yourself: "I did it! At first I was frustrated that I couldn't speak out, but I was able to stay focused on what he was saying and I could feel a strong connection. I practiced patience and focus and got all the way through the conversation without interrupting. I did it! And I am committed to not interrupting others so I can have greater connection."

> ## How to Give a Creative Recognition to Someone Else
>
> - Observe the person and when they are about to do exactly what they are supposed to do,
>
> - Make a request with which they are already on their way to complying. Voila! You've created a moment of success.
>
> - When requests are complied with, give plentiful acknowledgment in the form of Experiential Recognition: what values or qualities is the person upholding in his or her choices to comply with requests? Point out greatness qualities, character strengths, and virtues.
>
> ### For example:
>
> "Gloria, I know it has been hard for you to observe the No Texting While Driving law and I see that you are putting your cell phone out of reach before you even start the car. You are really working hard to develop a new good habit. Hooray for you! That shows me you are determined to obey the law and set a great example for your kids.
>
> You can also creatively recognize others as well as yourself for putting forth genuine effort, making difficult changes, overcoming obstacles, and staying on a trajectory of personal growth and ever- increasing achievement.

At times, due to time constraints, stress, emergencies, and the like, it's easy to get caught up in what is not done versus what is already accomplished or is being accomplished in that moment. By focusing on and appreciating positive accomplishments ***instead of worrying about or dwelling on what isn't done, you energize your desire to achieve.*** When your spirits are supported by positive recognitions, you will flourish creatively, intellectually, emotionally, and socially, and this comes back to benefit not only you but everyone in your life.

Creative Recognitions give you even more control over the flow of energy in your environment. Developing and living this practice, you begin to sense there is a cultural shift underway, and that the old paradigm of energy for negativity is being replaced with a positive flow of energy. Guide yourself to make ever more successful choices that support your growth as well as others in your life.

KEYS TO SUCCESSFUL CHANGE

Creative Recognition is one more tool that enables you to cultivate willingness, interests, and creativity by creating moments where success is inescapable—and then you give yourself or the deserving person all of the credit for that success.

Be a Nurtured Heart® Warrior

Consider the concept of The Nurtured Heart® Warrior who knows intuitively how to nurture hearts using all the Stands and Recognitions—and their commitment to doing so is upheld with warrior-like fierceness. You, too can be a Nurtured Heart Warrior®!

If the image of a warrior seems incongruent to you when thinking about a positive environment where everyone is flourishing, expand your understanding to include the total picture of a truly effective warrior. A warrior is much more than someone who learns to gain power over others through combat or warfare. The intense energy of a warrior can be channeled for peaceful purposes to gain influence with others.

A warrior's true essence is about being fearless in pursuit of goals—about courage, relentlessness, and achievement. Peace, perseverance, and hard work—the peaceful warrior's way—are the ways to reach one's goals. The spiritual warrior is on a quest for self-knowledge and the ability to serve others with this knowledge. As the leader who brings the Positivity Pulse to your life, you are stepping onto the path of the spiritual warrior.

NOTE: In a family or at school, workplace, or other community, use these strategies and be purposeful to honor those who are in compliance around the rule breaker. The rule breaker then begins to understand that rule compliance is what is energized. You will be amazed at how fast people shift their actions to adhere to the rule! For more "How To" in these situations, check out our other books at www.SherryBlairInstitute.com

Positivity Pulse Points

- **Choose values for your life that are in alignment with the way you want to live. These chosen values are like a beacon that pulls you ever closer to being the person you want to be.**

- Your chosen values serve as a foundation from which you build your personal rules or code of conduct. Precisely state your rules in the negative. For example, if one of your values is Integrity, you could have a rule that states: "No going back on my word."

- **Liberally give Proactive Recognitions to yourself by noticing and recognizing when you are not breaking rules. In doing this, you come to know success and feel an appreciation for living in alignment with your values.**

- Be as creative as possible in seeing opportunities to energize yourself for your positive choices. Energize each increment as you move in the direction of your values and goals.

- **Giving yourself energized recognitions of all types frequently throughout the day can create a flow of success and positivity, breaking down your resistance to change and opening your heart to a new and better way of relating to yourself and others.**

- Don't give up! If at first it seems awkward or silly, don't stop! Mastering this positive self-talk enables you to relate this way with others, too, thus deepening your relationships.

- **Be fearless and relentless in the pursuit of your goals to create more positive relationships where everyone flourishes!**

Create an action plan. Do it. No procrastinating. Make it happen.

ACTION STEP 1: Choose one rule you seem to have difficulty keeping. For example: "No texting while driving." Use Proactive Recognitions to notice and verbally acknowledge yourself when you are not breaking the rule. List the rule you will work with this week:

ACTION STEP 2: Practice giving Proactive Recognitions to your friends or family. Find at least one time EACH day this week when you can recognize a person out loud and in front of at least one other person. As you gain confidence in doing this, challenge yourself to giving a recognition in front of several people. Notice the reactions you experience and note below.

ACTION STEP 3: Choose one or two people who need to be drawn in a more successful direction. Energize them as often as possible with Creative Recognitions whenever you catch them about to break a rule they have trouble keeping so they get disrupted _before_ they do it. Then energize them afterward and name the difficulty they are having and give those heaps of recognition for complying.

Check your pulse.
Self-Assessment: Time to OPTIMIZE

Answer the following questions:

1. What did you set out to do by starting this Activity?

2. What did you accomplish?

3. What do you need to change to be the person you want to be?

4. What is the Pearl of Positivity Wisdom you received this week?

5. What is your OPTIMIZE Action Step that as the CEO (CHANGE-EXCEL-OPTIMIZE) in your life you will commit to for this upcoming week?

Optimize

ACTIVITY 7
Reset to OPTIMIZE:
Strategies to Get You Back on Track

Congratulations! What a long way you've come as you've been working to shift the energy in your life to radiate positivity! You've been learning and practicing so many ways to nurture yourself and to notice positivity flourishing in and around you. You know your values and your rules and you even know how to proactively acknowledge yourself for not breaking rules. You know how to build positivity in yourself and reinforce your good choices by creatively recognizing yourself when you are on the way to complying with a rule or value you have. But what do you do when you break a rule or do something out of alignment with your values? How do you get yourself back on track?

As an adult you might not have given much thought to resetting yourself, but you probably do know when you're not living your values or feel "stuck" in your life. How do you reset and nurture yourself at the same time?

Are you ready to find out? Let's go!

Activity 7 Objectives

- **To understand the power and energy of self-communication and how to use it effectively**

- **To learn to ask questions to determine whether you're thinking in a situation is rational and or irrational, and how to get yourself back on track if needed**

- **To discover your style for getting yourself back on track when you are not living your values or you've broken one of your personal rules and how giving "resets" can accelerate positivity for yourself as well as others**

- **To realize that celebrating small successes is an important part of broadening and building your overall success**

Activity 7 Summary

- **Thought and communication is energy. The communication you have with yourself is key to your success or failure.**

- **Whatever you think, your mind and body believes you. Questioning and correcting your negative thoughts will accelerate your success.**

- **A "reset" can be any word or signal you choose, as long as it holds the idea of pausing during a moment of rule-breaking and creating an opportunity to jump into a new moment of positivity. Sometimes you can even reset yourself and everyone back to a calm, peaceful state of being by taking just a moment of silence.**

- **Rational thinking moves us forward while irrational thinking keeps us stuck.**

Know What You Stand For...A Quick Review

In Activity 4 you established and gained a very clear understanding of which values are important to you. Let's look at the process that helped you define a positive foundation from which to nurture yourself:

- By choosing values that were important to you and doing the exercises you realized you needed to clearly state your values before you could create your personal code of conduct or commandments for how you want to live your life.

- Through understanding each value, you intuitively knew what the negatively stated rule should be that would uphold each of your values.

- Knowing your values is what creates buy-in for living in alignment with your rules and drives your decisions to make positive choices.

- Your decisions about how to live and nurture yourself are based on upholding your values and a need to get back on track stems from a disregard for those values.

Once you established or re-established your values and rules, they need to be clearly and strictly upheld by you in order to nurture yourself and live the way you desire. Here are several examples of personal code of conduct rules:

- No more being immediately available anytime someone texts, emails, messages

- No doing to others what I wouldn't do to myself.

- No ignoring my need for self-care—healthy eating, "me time," exercising, friendship and family time, sleep, hobbies, etc.

- No gossiping about other people
- No allowing myself to be disrespected or disrespecting others.

Change Starts with Awareness of Your Own Habits

To be effective at living in alignment with your values and to love and nurture yourself, you need to explore the ways in which negative behavior is enabled in your life first by your own behavior and then in your interactions with other people at home, work, and play.

Remember the caterpillars and butterflies from Step Two. Were there one or more characters you identified with? Any particular yucky habits you saw in them that you have? Note your answers here:

Ask yourself these questions to help you identify these habits:

- Do you have bad habits that you know you need to change – but don't?
- Have you cast a blind eye on a recurring problem?
- Have you been silent about a particular problem until it has happened so many times that you or someone else explodes with negative energy in reaction to it?
- Do you get special treatment and one-on-one attention behind closed doors when you break rules?
- Do you need a second person brought in to be the disciplinarian to set you straight?
- And since humans aren't perfect anyway, why do you need to be "set straight"? And why would you reset yourself??

It all goes back to your intention. The intention you set for yourself when you started this book. You know, the intention to take action to nurture yourself. That's what you were contemplating when you picked up this book in the first place. **Right???**

Right! So, if you don't remember your original intention, go back to Activity 1 and read the intention you wrote on page 19. (And if you have modified your original intention, use the current one.) Write it here:

Now, with your intention in mind it makes sense that you would want to reset yourself when you are not living in alignment with your intention. Sometimes you need a gentle reset to get you back on track with your intention and other times you need a good swift kick in your arse (as Sherry's Scottish grandmother would say). Whatever you need to do to make it happen, just do it. Be gentle. Be tough. Use humor. Whatever works for you but make it work.

So... when you find yourself living out of alignment with your values or breaking one of your commandments for living, what do you do?

How do you react?

What has been your habit of dealing with your own "non-compliance?"

Take an honest look before you go further.

Worksheet #15: "What Has Been My Style to Get Back on Track?"

Take a moment to think about how you have been dealing with your own rule-breaking and your reaction when you were not living in alignment with your values. How did you treat yourself? Self-blame, loathing, indifference, obsessing about it? Explore below how you have normally dealt with yourself and if/how you got back on track:

Value Ignored/Rule Broken

How I usually deal with myself to get back on track:

Value Ignored/Rule Broken

How I usually deal with myself to get back on track:

Value Ignored/Rule Broken

How I usually deal with myself to get back on track:

Resets

Now that you have explored how you used to discipline yourself when you were "off-track," let's look at some ways that you could "reset" yourself because staying on-track is a very important part of optimizing and nurturing yourself. Of course, "reset" isn't the only word that you could use. You could select a different word or a gesture that works for you. Have some fun and find a way that fits within your life at home, work and play. Even if it means running around blowing referee whistles, or holding a "reset" paddle up at home or work. **Bringing humor and laughter into a situation can ease the tension but be cautious when doing this toward someone else as it can come across in the wrong way.** "Recalculate" is a word that can remind you of your inner GPS—the part of you that knows how to calmly recalculate when you make a wrong turn and guides you back in the right direction. "Reboot" is a meaningful word techies understand and might like to use. There are other fun ways by using humor if that works for you, but by no means use sarcasm! Here are a few examples that we have learned from amazing people on our journey of guiding people toward reset:

- "I need a minute."

- A time out hand sign

- "I need to fall back" or "Let's all fall back."

- Remove yourself from the room with a polite way of excusing yourself.

- Even just being still and not pouncing on an opportunity to express your next thought can give you an opportunity to reset yourself without a word or a gesture. For those of you that are faith based, or spiritual, think about your faith and trusting in that energy.

It doesn't matter which one you decide on as long as you understand what it means. And if you are going to use resets on someone other than yourself, make sure you share the concept with them and choose a word/gesture that works for everyone. **Don't just go along resetting people without understanding its power because abusing it or misusing it can have a very negative impact and that's not the goal.**

For now, let's use the word "reset." Think of it as a keyword that supports you in ridding yourself of a negative cognition, negative behavior, or an unhealthy negative thought or emotion that arises as a knee-jerk reaction to some negativity or breaking a rule. Using resets gives you an opportunity to remind yourself and those in your life that you (or they) can reset away from negativity as soon as you realize it is happening.

Refuse to give your precious energy to problems—your pitfalls included. In this approach, we use a "reset" as an immediate response to breaking a rule. A reset is about taking a stand to enforce your personal code for living.

And why would you use a reset on yourself?? Because in nurturing yourself you are saying ***YES YES YES*** to living your values in rational and positive ways and ***NO NO NO*** to unhealthy negativity and self-defeating behaviors. You are increasing your belief in yourself and living the life you want to live. It's about standing strong in your conviction! It's about communicating to others in your circles.

- NO unhealthy negative emotion.
- NO irrational thinking.
- NO self-defeating behavior.
- NO toxic people in your life.

Refuse to be sucked into creating negative energy around problems, doubts, and worries. Instead, set your intention to create a positive environment where you want to be. When you have challenges, practice shifting your energy away from negativity by finding a way to create success in that moment.

Reflect on Baby Steps.

Sometimes you may have to drop the expectation as low as necessary and champion each minute of success to create more success.

Basically, resetting yourself involves simply resetting your own thoughts or negative behavior away from negativity using self-communication.

Let's explore this powerful concept.

The Power of Self-Communication

Did you know every cell in your body believes what you tell yourself? Your energy is affected by your thoughts. The communication you have with yourself is key to your success or failure. You really need to block out negative and irrational thinking in order to help free yourself of thoughts that drag you down. Your mindset, your blood flow – everything is healthier when you are rational, calm and in control. We like to tell the teenagers that we work with that you are safe, smart and in charge when you are calm and in control. You are guiding the success in your life. Again, your thoughts have tremendous power! Every cell in your body believes what you tell yourself, as your energy is affected by your thoughts. The communication you have with yourself is key to your success or failure.

Most people do not understand how important thoughts are and leave the development of thought patterns to chance. Did you know that every thought you have sends electrical signals throughout your brain? Research has shown that thoughts have actual physical properties. They are real! They have significant influence on every cell in your body. When you just think a negative thought without challenging it, your mind believes it and your body reacts to it.

"If you think you can do a thing or you think you can't do a thing, you are right."

~ Henry Ford

What a powerful statement! Thoughts have so much power over us. And so many of our thought are irrational!

Which Do You Choose?

Thinking back to your original intention from Activity 1, when you find your thoughts/behavior/actions are not in support of that intention, ask yourself these powerful questions:

- Does this get me closer to my intention or further away?
- Do I want to make a change or stay as I am?

- Which do I choose: flourishing or languishing? Do I want to grow and blossom or wilt and starve to death?

- Success or failure?

- Win or lose?

- Am I moving or procrastinating?

Irrational Thinking and Self-sabotaging Behaviors

Although adults would seem to be too mature to act out to get attention in the ways a child would do, this isn't always the case. Be honest and relentless with yourself to determine if you are acting out childish patterns of behavior, using self-sabotaging behavior, or thinking negative or irrational thoughts. Some adults even seem to thrive on negative attention and all the drama that surrounds it.

Let's take a look at some popular patterns of irrational thinking to see how you may be self-sabotaging your progress and how you can make changes.

Awfulizing

Stop with the drama kings and queens! "This is terrible, that's horrible – it's awful." Think about what's really terrible in the world! You know, 9/11 – that was pretty terrible. The Holocaust - pretty horrific. Abuse and neglect of children and adults, racism – those kinds of things are truly awful. But some people, as you know, make a mountain out of a mole-hill. Saying things like, "Oh this is the worst thing in the world that could've happened to me!" Typically, there is usually something *much* worse that could happen to you! So stop awfulizing things! Stop making things more dramatic than they need to be! That leads to unhealthy negative emotions, which then leads to self-defeating behaviors because awfulizing creates irrational beliefs and ruminating thought patterns. Learn to increase your frustration tolerance by using the "Then what?" method.

When you find yourself awfulizing, stop your downward spiral of negativity and turn it around by asking "And then what?" Continue asking "And then what?" after each of your answers until you see that it really would not be the end of the world. By doing this exercise whenever you fall into the downward spiral of irrational thinking, you will train yourself to move up out of that pit and into rational thinking mode. And when you are thinking rationally, you will be able to summon the energy to creatively think of positive action you could take, and have the energy to follow through.

The Worst That Can Happen...

What if you feel you just can't face someone? The truth is you can face anybody. You really can. You may not prefer it but you can handle it. You are not going to crumble. We do a lot of rational emotive behavioral coaching or therapy and one thing we are trained to teach people is to think about what is the worst thing that could happen.

For example, someone might be losing his or her home. That's a pretty sucky thing to happen. But if the worst thing was that you lost it and then you had to rent an apartment, you could tolerate it. You could definitely move on and live your life. Even though it would be sad and unfortunate to lose the home, the truth is you would still be able to find another place to live and create another home. So stop saying, "I can't stand this" or "I can't stand that," because when you do, you allow your negative self-talk to keep you stuck. Your frustration tolerance stays very, very low and your patience stays really low and you don't have the energy to pick yourself up and take ACTION.

Whenever you find yourself engaging in this type of talk, employ the "And then what?" method to bring you back to rational thinking so you can think more clearly and make an action plan for yourself.

Giving Up Too Soon

And if you tend to get frustrated and quit trying before you find success by saying something like, "I can't stand it!" I just can't stand it, I must be awful because I can't seem to make it happen" remember the quote above from Henry Ford. Quit telling yourself you can't! If you fail at your task, just analyze it to see where you made a mistake and learn from it. Then try it again. Remember Edison who tried 10,000 ways to make the electric light bulb. In his mind he hadn't "failed" 10,000 times; he just found 10,000 ways that did not work to make the light bulb, and learned from each mistake and tried again until he found success.

So if you're wanting to give up and throw in the towel, take another look, analyze what you are trying to do, and look for the missing steps or learning you need to get to be successful and TRY AGAIN!

Judgment

Rating yourself and others creates barriers to unconditional connection and compassion. Have you heard that we humans form a first impression of someone in 10 seconds? We are wired to make judgments, and sometimes it's true that making a snap judgment can save our lives, but most of the time we tend to rush to judgment when it's not necessary. Cultivate a curious inquiring mind. Open your heart, ask questions, and look for the value in each person or situation. Don't judge others. Do not judge others!

And don't be so hard on yourself! None of us is perfect. Don't say "I'm bad." Let's say a relationship ends, and you start putting yourself down: "Why?" "What did I do?" "There must be something wrong with me." Right? People do that all the time. That doesn't help the situation.

Procrastination

Procrastinating is a self-defeating behavior--it's when we keep putting things off. And since procrastination is such a big factor that contributes to NOT getting what you want, let's look at tips to get moving here.

When you feel yourself wanting to put something off until later, think about your choices and your *why*. This helps drive you to get started. Studies show the most difficult part of getting something done is *starting*. So get out your calendar and put in your start dates and finish deadline and also calendar for the major steps you need to accomplish in order to keep moving toward your goal.

When you are thinking about your choices, think about your vision. Feel it. Picture your vision several times a day to engage your heart and brain and spirit to keep you moving forward.

Marshall your resources, especially if you need outside help or have to learn something new in order to get it done. Engage your values and your strengths to help you.

Celebrate each success along the way no matter how small. Yes! Give yourself recognitions as you have learned and celebrate all along the way. Use these tips to lift yourself up with positivity and you will sail through to your goal!

Unconditional

You also need to eliminate globally rating of self and others to nurture yourself. Everyone is human and fallible. We all make mistakes. We all live and grow at different paces. Rational thinking involves unconditional self-acceptance and unconditional acceptance of others and unconditional acceptance that life happens. When you realize those things unconditionally, you will be able to deal with whatever is happening – especially in the face of adversity or a crisis.

Think of a situation that happened in your life that you "awfulized" that it was soooo bad, or the worst that could happen and how it didn't turn out as bad as you thought it would. Notice how worrying didn't solve the problem, but when you look back, the situation definitely could have been worse.

How could you have used rational thinking and resetting yourself to help keep your mind serene during that situation?

How do you think this would have improved the situation?

Imposing Values

In the mental health field as well as in coaching and training, we have to consider if we are imposing our values on someone else. Other people have a right to their own values and it's not your job to police or bully them. You only get to choose what's right for you.

For example, one person's value might be to have a home that is in order, while somebody else might live in a very messy place based on others' standards, yet each place may not be comfortable for another person based on someone else's standards. If they are okay with it, that's up to them—that is their right.

Don't impose your values on others and don't try to change someone to fit your standards. Of course we can always strive to support someone who chooses to make changes, but it must be *their* choice and *their* efforts or it won't happen. Even as parents try to impart their values on their children, it doesn't always happen that all their children choose all their values. Parents especially know that each person is unique. ☺

To reset to positivity

- Stop saying "This is the worst thing that can happen."

- Stop being so dramatic. Take a few deep breaths to calm yourself down and get some much-needed oxygen to your brain and train yourself to ask: "And if this bad thing happens, then what?"

- Keep asking yourself "Then what?" after each answer until you see that it really would not be the end of the world. By doing this exercise whenever you fall into the downward spiral of irrational thinking, you will train yourself to move up out of that pit and into rational thinking mode. And when you are thinking rationally, you will be able to summon the energy to creatively think of positive action you could take, and have the energy to follow through.

- Stop rating yourself and others.

- Don't compare yourself to others. Don't seek out the approval of others. You are unique and have your own value.

- Don't say "I'm bad." Let's say a relationship ends, and you start putting yourself down: "Why?" "What did I do?" "There must be something wrong with me." Right? People do that all the time. That doesn't help the situation.

- Don't judge others. Do not judge others!

- Increase your frustration tolerance – stop saying "I can't stand it!"

- Don't impose your values on others – you have to be very mindful of that. Other people have a right to their own values and it's not your job to police or bully them. You only get to choose what's right for you.

- Keep trying and learn from your mistakes.

- Don't compare yourself to others. Don't seek out the approval of others. You are unique and have your own value.

- Practice unconditional self-acceptance and unconditional acceptance of others and unconditional acceptance that life happens.

- Push yourself to move and win now! Set a deadline for yourself.

- Don't impose your values on others or try to change them to fit your standards.

"When you are honest with yourself and observe your irrational thinking and behavior patterns clearly, you'll see they drive all your decisions. And they also give you clues for when it's time to reset yourself."

~sherry blair

Back to Resets

Challenging conversations can be a great place to practice resetting yourself. Yes, that's right – even in the heat of the moment. When you do this, even in challenging conversations, effective communication is the result – if you are unconditionally accepting of yourself, unconditionally accepting of others as human beings that make mistakes and see them at that heart and soul level, your communication is going to be sooooo much better. Even if you have to say something that another person doesn't want to hear, the truth is it will come from a place of compassion because you're in healthy control of yourself and all because you chose to reset for optimization.

When resetting, realize that it's a process and not automatic like turning a light switch on and off. It can be really hard to do but with practice you'll get better and better at it and it will be a faster process down the road. Here are some tips to help you reset back to your intention:

- Hold your vision clearly in your mind and in your heart. Think about it in detail and imagine what it would feel like to be that now. Do this several times a day to reinforce and anchor your intention.

- What is your "WHY?" What is your reason and compelling vision?

- What would you have to do more of to make it a reality?

- What would you have to stop doing to allow it to happen?

- Be self-aware to notice if you are really practicing this new approach with consistency.

- Be determined and relentless

- Practice using your new tools and challenge yourself to become skillful

- As a role model for those around you, set the expectations and the standards yourself

So, what are you going to stop doing by resetting yourself? What is standing in the way of nurturing your heart and Optimizing YOU? Name three things here. (But one is OK, too.)

1.

2.

3.

Worksheet #16: "Reset the Nurtured Heart® Way"

One of the most powerful uses of the reset is in resetting your own thoughts or negative behavior away from negativity. Practice resetting yourself before you put some negative thoughts into words or a sarcastic text, voicemail, email or exchange in a conversation. Being a role model for this practice is key to making this transformation in your life at home, work and play.

Let everyone around you know you're just as prepared to reset yourself as you are to reset them. Say it out loud: "Oops! Time to reset myself!" And then take yourself and your tribe right back to the beat of the Positivity Pulse. Whatever the case, list a few examples below and commit to resetting yourself when you catch negativity brewing.

Go back and look at Worksheet 14 to review what you wrote down about what you have been doing. It's time for the new Nurtured Heart® way. Let's explore what you are going to do from this day forward.

<u>Values Ignored/Rule Broken</u>

With your new knowledge, what are you committing to as your new Nurtured Heart® way to reset yourself?

What techniques are you going to try?

What new things resonated with you the most?

Strive for Rational Thinking

Now here is where you can change your language to help you change your thoughts – here is where you can get rid of the musts, the absolutes and the shoulds. Instead say things like: "I wish it would have happened like this," or "I would have liked for this to happen" or "I prefer." These are your preferences and when you can think about what your preferences are, such as "I would prefer that all of my goals this year are met," then you are practicing rational thinking skills. **You are optimizing!!!**

It's not that you won't think about "should haves" or "musts" ever again—believe me, you are likely to, especially when something is very important to you or emotionally charged. But you can quickly use these new skills you are learning to reset and realize that it's okay and you will know with a strong belief within you that you can handle it. "I would just prefer it. But it doesn't have to happen."

When you are evaluating "badness" versus "awfulizing," when you are making something dramatic and terrible and awful – try these phrases instead: "Well this is pretty bad" or "It could be worse" or "It's unfortunate." When you think about these things, when something happens to you, it's important to count your blessings. You can find reasons to be thankful even in a sometimes pretty cruddy situation. "It's unfortunate, but I can get through it and perhaps it could have been worse."

Strive for rational thinking! Increase to a higher frustration tolerance! "I can deal with this." "I can stand it." In the example of someone who was going to maybe lose their home—which many people in America have in economic downturns --this is something that many people have strong emotional ties to. The truth is, you would be able to deal with it and you would end up getting an apartment or sharing a place and making a new home. Who knows what the horizon would have in store for you? You need to believe that you can work through it and you can deal with it. Sometimes one door has to close for others to open.

Even people who have survived a car accident and are suffering with post-traumatic stress symptoms may say, "You know I really can't get into a car again" which is the furthest thing from the truth because they *can* get in a car again. And they actually *did* deal with it! They made it through the car accident, right? When they start looking at these kinds of statements, "Well I made it through the worst part, I can certainly do this again. I have driven for years and didn't have an accident. It is not statistically reasonable to say I will have another car accident like that any time soon,"- that's when they start using rational thinking and increase their frustration tolerance.

Broaden and Build

Barbara Fredrickson's terrific research on Positivity tells us about the Positivity Ratio – you need a ratio of three or more positive things to every negative thing in order to counterbalance the negativity and to feel positive overall. (Yes, it's true. Negativity is "heavier" than positivity and pulls us down more, so we need a higher positivity ratio to fuel positivity.) Knowing this concept can really help you as you practice the strategies to nurture yourself. In the Nurtured Heart Approach®, we refer to this as your Inner Wealth™. When we work on increasing positivity, research studies show amazing things happen within us.

> *We are building up our internal resources and*
> *guess when they come in really handy?*
> *Yup, you got it, in times of crisis, adversity and especially*
> *when it is Time to RESET!*

In order to broaden and build your positivity and accelerate your self-nurturing with the strategies you've learned in this program make sure you give yourself lots of enthusiastic recognitions for:

- All the good things you are thinking/feeling/doing (Active Recognitions)
- The good values you are demonstrating (Experiential Recognitions)
- All the bad things that you aren't doing that you could be doing (Proactive Recognitions)
- And the good things you are about to do (Creative Recognitions)

Celebrating is Part of Your Self-Nurturing

Celebrate your successes no matter how big or how small. Nurture yourself! Feel your success in your heart. Let those good feelings stream through your body. Why not? When you see other people doing well, you give them a high five, right? You're excited for them! You see athletes doing it all the time! Think about when somebody comes across that finish line – everybody is there for that high five or great big hug.

So nurture yourself! You deserve it! Indulge in giving yourself that high five. Notice your success – this is a key thing. How many times have we repeated it? It's pretty important. Remember to anchor it in psychologically, emotionally, physically, spiritually and energetically. Notice it in your body. How does it feel when you've completed a task? Regardless of what it is, how does it feel? Even by doing these steps, you are learning! Give yourself credit!

- Think about how light your energy feels when you are moving towards your success. If you're a spiritual person, anchor this in spiritually: pray on it, ask for whatever it is that you need to be successful.

- Look in the mirror and give yourself a high-five. Or ten!

- Do it on an hourly basis at first. Use the recognitions you have learned and you will find lots of things to celebrate even every hour. BUILD YOUR POSITIVITY!

- If need be, set a timer on your phone. In the beginning, you might not be used to this new practice – this new way of noticing yourself. So try having your timer go off every hour - just a little "ding" - and tell yourself what's going well in the moment.

- Even if you're at work – you showed up for work and you're getting your work done! Perhaps that is going to help you succeed in whatever goal you set out for yourself.

Think about your high five and give yourself credit!

Feel it! Know it! Believe it!

Benefits of Rational Thinking: Clear Blue Sky Thinking

The benefits of rational thinking, which we like to call "Clear Blue Sky Thinking," come when you maintain healthy negative emotions and do not allow them to become all-consuming or destructive. Here are some examples:

- Healthy anger does not turn into rage.

- Disappointment, loss and grief, sadness does not turn into depression.

- Concern does not turn into worry or anxiety.

- Healthy shame and guilt does not turn into self-loathing.

Maintaining healthy negative emotion is what you want. You eliminate self-defeating behaviors – ideally. Even if you don't completely eliminate them, you want to decrease self-defeating behaviors. Anything that prevents you from goal attainment, such as procrastinating or not working on it every day or every week at least – is a self-defeating behavior. Anything that keeps you from nurturing yourself is a self-defeating behavior. You need to reveal to yourself what exactly is holding you back and this happens in the process of resetting.

Also, if you have irrational thoughts such as "Oh, I should have been here ten years ago," well that and five cents won't even get you a phone call! That's not going to be helpful, and then you kind of get stuck. You want to think rationally because it helps you maintain healthy negative emotions while self-defeating behaviors are decreased. Resetting keeps your mind calm and serene. Calm and peaceful minds prevail. Your cellular health is better off. You relate positively with yourself and others. Relationships flourish at home, work and play. You have more patience. You are not on edge – you are calm, you are in a good place, you are in healthy control of yourself.

Reset Yourself in Challenging Conversations

When you do this, even in challenging conversations, effective communication is the result – if you are unconditionally accepting of yourself, unconditionally accepting of others as human beings that make mistakes and see them at that heart and soul level, your communication is going to be sooooo much better. Even if you have to say something that another person doesn't want to hear, the truth is it will come from a place of compassion because you're in healthy control of yourself and all because you chose to reset for optimization.

KEYS TO SUCCESSFUL CHANGE

Be self-aware to notice if you are really practicing this new approach with consistency.

- **Be relentless.**

- **Be determined.**

- **Practice using your new tools and challenge yourself to become skillful.**

- **As a role model for those around you, you set the expectations and the standards.**

Positivity Pulse Points

- **Change begins with awareness of and examination of your own habits. Be aware of negative habits, behaviors or ways of thinking that you want to eliminate and work to reset yourself before you get too far afield.**

- When you are living out of alignment with your values or breaking your personal code of conduct, you can reset yourself to get back on track.

- **The communication you have with yourself is key to your success or failure. You really need to block out negative and irrational thinking in order to help free yourself of thoughts that drag you down.**

- Refuse to relapse into your old habits of creating negative energy around problems, doubts, and worries. Instead, set your intention to create a positive and peaceful environment both internally and externally.

- **When you have challenges, practice shifting your energy away from negativity by finding a way to create success in that moment.**

- If you find yourself falling into the downward spiral of irrational thinking, quickly employ your new strategies of self-communication and questioning to move up out of that pit and into rational thinking mode. Then you will be able to summon the energy to creatively think of positive action you could take, and have the energy to follow through.

- **Celebrate yourself by recognizing your successes no matter how large or small. Make a habit of doing it once an hour in the beginning so you amp up your positivity!**

Create an action plan. Do it. No procrastinating. Make it happen.

ACTION STEP 1: Decide on what word, gesture or phrase you will use to reset yourself and write it here.

ACTION STEP 2: List one or two ways you enable negativity in your life and then list strategies you can employ to eliminate it.

ACTION STEP 3: Set alarms on your phone or other electronic device to go off at regular times during your day so that you can recognize yourself for what is going right in the moment.

RESET TO STOP THE INSANITY SUCCESS STORY

As a mental health professional and coach, I am quite fortunate because I am continuously surrounded by amazing life changing techniques to increase success in life, personal and professional well-being and overall happiness. That sounds pretty good, doesn't it? But the truth is, I come to the table, just like anyone else, with my ups and downs, my great characteristics and the ones I would prefer not to acknowledge or may be denying that I even have. I know that I had a pretty solid foundation of amazing techniques before I learned about the Nurtured Heart Approach®. The one that I thought aligned in such a powerful way was positive psychology which I was living and breathing and trying to find ways to make it come alive in my personal life and in practice.

Finding NHA, was like finding the golden key to open up that universe because it is specific and it is the "how" which is embodied in the precision tools that it offers. I was beyond thrilled when I learned about it but looking back, finding it also meant I would go through some painful experiences if I was going to apply it in my life. You see, I am a big believer in NOT being a hypocrite—I wholeheartedly apply the things I teach to others and to myself. In my experience, I have witnessed many mental health professionals being great at telling others they need therapy, but often refuse to see their own need for therapy or coaching. I don't agree with that style. So here I am amped up to infuse NHA in my organization and also began using it on myself in my personal relationships. When I first read Glasser's *You Are Oprah* book, I began using it with the people I served and applying it in my personal life.

Using it in my personal life meant I had to get real honest about my behavior that was truly enabling ongoing dysfunction in my relationship with my adult son and in my romantic relationship at that time. While my intentions were authentic in wanting to help and support them both as they were clearly going through tough times and inner turmoil, the truth is I was avoiding confrontation; I was turning a blind eye to what they were doing; and I was allowing emotional and sometimes verbal abuse spearheaded for me. Stand one—refusing to give energy to negativity and Stand Three—having limits and realizing what the consequences are was something I was not good at and while I had also employed energy psychology in my life, I still had no clue how to stop what was happening—until I found the NHA. I was able to shine the light on their wonderful qualities but I was failing miserably on how to stop the insanity I was living at that time. Applying NHA in my life did in turn improve my relationship with my son and allowed me to show him how to start loving and forgiving himself for past mistakes because I was role modeling how to love and respect myself. Sadly, it didn't work that way with my ex-boyfriend and we parted ways—tearfully but with a true sense of knowing that making that step was setting me free—I was stuck in the chrysalis for a long time and I was struggling to break free to spread my wings to soar. The NHA helped me to transform to be a better version of myself. A similar version of this story happened in our workplace too—I realized that being relentless with NHA also meant that STOPPING the insanity meant letting go of some people in my life and at work—even if you cared very deeply for them.

sherry blair

Check your pulse.
Self-Assessment: Time to OPTIMIZE

Answer the following questions:

1. What did you set out to do by starting this Activity?

2. What did you accomplish?

3. What do you need to change to be the person you want to be?

4. What is the Pearl of Positivity Wisdom you received this week?

5. What is your OPTIMIZE Action Step that as the CEO (CHANGE-EXCEL-OPTIMIZE) in your life you will commit to for this upcoming week?

Our Wish For You

Be Your Authentic Self

As you are at the end of this self-coaching leg of your journey, don't let it be an end, but rather the beginning of your newly-nurtured authentic self. Hold these words close to your heart and repeat often. Let the words wash over you as you say them out loud or silently:

> *"I am unique.*
> *No one has ever lived with my set of circumstances and*
> *my unique experiences and my unique gifts.*
> *I am here to learn to love and nurture myself so that*
> *I can love and nurture others and share my unique gifts."*

You need to believe in yourself and what you are doing in order to nurture yourself and spiral up your positivity. It's all about your self-communication.

- What are you telling yourself?
- If you don't believe that you can be it or do it, you won't.
- You need to believe it and you need to remove the clutter that gets in your way when you have those moments of self-doubt.

We Get Off Track Too

We are achieving and doing things all the time and we can personally tell you at times, those little creepy demons come in and we're like "no, no, no!" So, it's really important to remember and **PRACTICE** the tools and strategies you've learned in this guide and know when to flip that switch to clear those cognitive distortions out of your mind, which will help you stay on track with your intentions – whatever they may be. This way you're able to communicate your vision to others. Tune in to your self-communication and be your authentic self and be authentic with others. To be successful, be mindful of your habits. You really need to practice walking the talk. Some people talk the talk or walk the walk, but we want you to walk the talk. Be your authentic self. ☺

Our wish for you is that these tools and strategies and positive self-communication will become a part of your authentic self – the best version of yourself, your heart-felt self, and that you will continue to nurture yourself and others and grow into your highest potential.

Serenity Mantra

Congratulations! You've come so far and grown so much! Give yourself a lot of credit for that! Put your hands on your heart and feel the beat of positivity – your positivity pulse! Stand up straight and give yourself a big hug!

We'd like to share this Serenity Prayer with you as it is a favorite of ours. If you are not religious, when you remove the word God, it allows everyone to appreciate the words, as well as respect whether you have a higher power or not. Some of you who are spiritual or religious in certain religions may already know this mantra. That's beautiful – go with that. Put the name of your higher power in the beginning of it as a prayer form if that's what works for you. But if that's not what works for you, that's neither here nor there! It's the words that are the meaning.

> ## "Grant me the serenity to accept the things I cannot change, the courage to change the things that I can and the wisdom to know the difference."

It's a beautiful and calming mantra to say when you're faced with a challenging time. You can actually just say these few words and it can help you to re-center and move forward. So, we hope that you get something out of it as well. If need be, write it down and keep it with you. Or better yet, find one that works for you and ***make it work!***

For personal and professional coaching and training, check our website at

Institute For
Inspirational Change

SherryBlairInstitute.com

About the Authors

Alletta Bayer

As the Chief Product Officer and Master Trainer at the Sherry Blair Institute for Inspirational Change, Alletta is passionate about developing and delivering curricula for personal and professional development and greater well-being. Alletta champions lifelong learning and constantly draws from research in positive psychology, human behavior, neurobiology, epigenetics and nutrition therapy to create compelling and relevant trainings to help people create the change they want to see.

Alletta is the co-author along with Sherry Blair of *The 7 Steps to Ignite Flourishing Leaders, Teams and Organizations.* She is a contributor to *The 8 Steps to Lead Change in Your Life* and *The Power to Change.*

She is a California licensed marriage and family therapist (LMFT) and holds numerous certifications including Advanced Trainer/Certified Nurtured Heart Specialist, Certified High Performance Coach (one of 300 in the world trained by Brendon Burchard), Dr. Amen Certified Brain Health Coach, and Certified Gluten Practitioner. Alletta is a graduate of the Professional Coaching Course trained by founder, James Flaherty. She served on the inaugural Global Summit Committee for the Children's Success Foundation for the Nurtured Heart Approach®.

Alletta graduated with a BA from University of California, Berkeley and a MA in Clinical Psychology from John F. Kennedy University.

SherryBlairInstitute.com

Sherry Blair

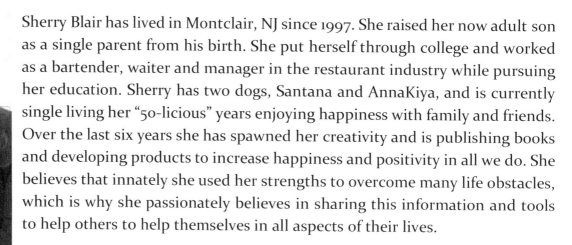

Sherry Blair has lived in Montclair, NJ since 1997. She raised her now adult son as a single parent from his birth. She put herself through college and worked as a bartender, waiter and manager in the restaurant industry while pursuing her education. Sherry has two dogs, Santana and AnnaKiya, and is currently single living her "50-licious" years enjoying happiness with family and friends. Over the last six years she has spawned her creativity and is publishing books and developing products to increase happiness and positivity in all we do. She believes that innately she used her strengths to overcome many life obstacles, which is why she passionately believes in sharing this information and tools to help others to help themselves in all aspects of their lives.

As CEO/Founder of Sherry Blair Institute for Inspirational Change, Sherry inspires and motivates others by applying and encouraging Positive Psychology, Rational Emotive Behavior Skills and the Nurtured Heart Approach. She uses her skills to teach others how to build effective teams, and use non-violent communication to achieve results and resolve conflict. Teaching others to speak from their hearts is a key constituent of the work she does.

Sherry is a graduate of Rutgers University with a Bachelor of Arts in Psychology and Women's Studies. She went on to obtain her Masters of Science in Social Work with a concentration in Policy Analysis and International Social Welfare at Columbia University. She is dually mastered in Industrial and Organizational Psychology supporting her vision to make change at the macro level in leadership and management. Sherry teaches part-time as an adjunct assistant professor for the University of Southern California in their virtual academic center in the Graduate School of Social Work. She teaches Human Behavior in the Social Environment and Consultation, Coaching and Social Entrepreneurship.

Sherry is a New Jersey Licensed Clinical Social Worker, a Board Certified Professional Counselor and an IABMCP Professional Coach. Sherry is one of the first 300 in the world to be trained by Dr. Martin Seligman in his Vanguard Authentic Happiness Positive Psychology Coaching Program. She is also advanced trained in evidence based Rational Emotive Behavior Therapy (REBT)/Coaching and was privileged to be trained by Albert Ellis who is considered one of the greatest psychologists of our time. She is an Advanced Trainer/Certified Nurtured Heart Specialist and has served on the Ethics & Global Summit Committees for the Children's Success Foundation and The Nurtured Heart Approach®, a transformational approach that changes lives.

References

Bayer, Alletta & Blair, Sherry. *7 Steps to Ignite Flourishing in Leaders, Teams & Organizations.* New Jersey: Shakti Publishing. 2013.

Blair, Sherry. *OPTIMIZE: Leading Change In Your Life.* New Jersey: Shakti Publishing. 2015

Blair, Sherry, and Melissa Lynn Block. *The Positivity Pulse: Transforming Your Workplace.* New Jersey: Shakti Publishing, 2011. 1-114.

Ellis, Albert. *Feeling Better, Getting Better, Staying Better: Profound Self-help Therapy for Your Emotions.* Atascadero, California: Impact Publishers, 2001. 1-272.

Fredrickson, Barbara L. 2004. "The Broaden-and-Build Theory of Positive Emotions." *Philosophical Transactions: Biological Sciences,* 2004. 1367. JSTOR *Journals,* EBSCO*host* (accessed August 5, 2015)

Glasser, Howard. *Igniting Greatness: Remembering Who You Are Through the Nurtured Heart Approach.* Arizona: Center of the Difficult Child. 2015.

Glasser, Howard. *You Are Oprah: Igniting Fires of Greatness.* Arizona: Center of the Difficult Child. 2009.

Kotter, John P. *A Sense of Urgency.* Boston, Massachusetts: Harvard Business Press, 2008. 1-208.

Lyubomirsky, Sonja. *The How of Happiness: A Scientific Approach to Getting the Life You Want.* New York, New Jersey: Penguin Press, 2008. 1-384.

Lyubomirsky, Sonja, Kennon M. Sheldon, and David Schkade. "Pursuing Happiness: The Architecture of Sustainable Change." *Review of General Psychology* 9, no. 2 (2005): 111-31.

Lyubomirsky, Sonja, Rene Dickerhoof, Julia K. Boehm, and Kennon M. Sheldon. "Becoming Happier Takes Both a Will and a Proper Way: An Experimental Longitudinal Intervention to Boost Well-being." *Emotion* 11, no. 2 (2011): 391-402.

Peterson, Christopher & Seligman, Martin. *Character Strengths and Virtues: A Handbook and Classification.* American Psychological Association. New York: Oxford University Press. 2004.

Seligman, Martin. *Flourish: A Visionary Understanding of Happiness and Well-Being.* New York: Atria Books. 2012.

Create a POSITIVITY PULSE @ Home, Work & Play

With Alletta Bayer and Sherry Blair

For Organizations

Blair, Sherry with Melissa Lynn Block (2011). ***The Positivity Pulse: Transforming Your Workplace.*** (English Edition).

Blair, Sherry with Luis Fernandez (2012). ***El Pulso De La Pulso: Transformando Su Lugar De Trabajo.*** (Spanish Edition)

Blair, Sherry (2013). Creative Recognitions, Inc.: ***Flourish Vs. Languish: Which Side Are You On?***

Create a POSITIVITY PULSE @ Home, Work & Play
With Alletta Bayer and Sherry Blair

For Adults

Blair, Sherry (2015). **OPTIMIZE: Leading Change In Your Life.** (With Special Contributions by Alletta Bayer & Roxanne Miller)

Bayer, Alletta & Blair, Sherry (2016). **OPTIMIZE: 7 Simple Steps to Nurture Your Heart.**

Create a POSITIVITY PULSE @ Home, Work & Play
With Ailetta Bayer and Sherry Blair

For Children & Teens/Parents & Professionals

Blair, Sherry & Bonilla, Nancy Azevedo (2013). ***Jangala Tribal Warriors: Living, Growing and Learning From the Heart.*** (English Edition)

Blair, Sherry & Bonilla, Nancy Azevedo (2013). ***Guerreros Tribales de Jangala: Amando, Creciendo y Aprendiendo Desde el Corazon.*** (Spanish/English Edition)

Blair, Sherry & Bonilla, Nancy Azevedo (To Be Released 2016). ***Jangala Tribal Warriors: A World Full Of Greatness.***

Blair, Sherry & Bonilla, Nancy Azevedo & Hollywood-Lehman, Kelly (2013). ***The Facilitator's Guide for Jangala Tribal Warriors: Living, Growing and Learning From The Heart.***

Create a POSITIVITY PULSE
@ Home, Work & Play

With Alletta Bayer and Sherry Blair

Blair, Sherry with Lofrano, ToniAnne (2013). *Tribal Warriors: Life Skills To Optimize Well-Being For Teens/Creating Nurtured Heart Communities.*

All books are available on amazon.com and barnesandnoble.com. Contact us directly at info@sherryblairinstitute.com for bulk rates, live and virtual trainings. For more information, check out our websites at www.SherryBlairInstitute.com

SherryBlairInstitute.com

The Nurtured Heart Approach®

And

Children's Success Foundation

The Nurtured Heart Approach (NHA) is a proven relationship-based method that guides children to use their intensity in positive and healthy ways. Originally developed for working with the most challenging children, NHA awakens the greatness in all children and supports them in developing their own Inner Wealth®.

Rather than acting out negatively, children begin to act out their greatness and adults get to experience the joy of being a highly effective agent of change in the lives of children.

In addition to supporting all children to flourish, NHA creates transformative changes in children who are behaviorally, emotionally, socially and academically challenged, including children with diagnoses like:

*Attention Deficit/Hyperactivity Disorder (ADHD)

*Oppositional Defiant Disorder (ODD)

*Reactive Attachment Disorder (RAD)

*Autism Spectrum Disorder (ASD)

*Asperger Syndrome (AS)

*Anxiety Disorders

*Self-Harm

*Bullying

NHA is a powerful tool that creates enduring and successful transformation in all children.

Children's Success Foundation is a non-profit organization that promotes the Nurtured Heart Approach through on-line training and live presentations. For more information go to

www.childrenssuccessfoundation.com

Made in the USA
Columbia, SC
11 July 2020